ULTRARUNN
EUROPE

EXPLORATIONS OF EUROPEAN
LONG DISTANCE AND EXTREME TRAILS
THROUGH RUNNING

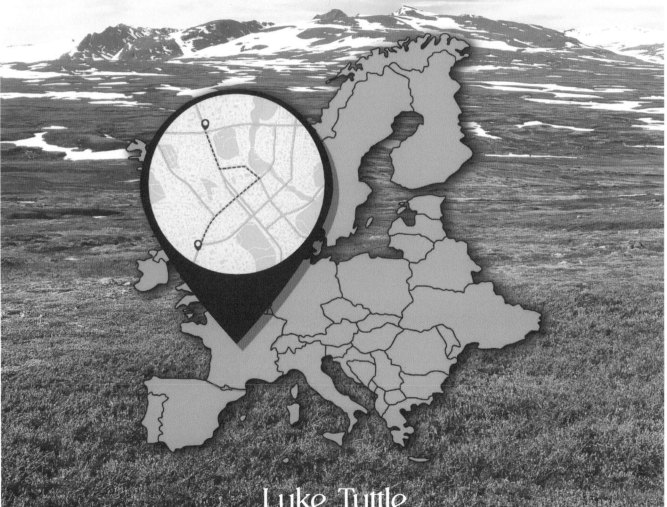

Luke Tuttle

ACKNOWLEDGEMENTS: Map data from © OpenStreetMap (openstreetmap.org/copyright)

ISBN: 979-8-9882949-0-0

E-mail: ultrarunningdestinations@gmail.com

Photography: Luke Tuttle
Composition: Luke Tuttle
Writing: Luke Tuttle

FOREWORD

You might be surprised that the author of this book is not from Europe. Instead, I'm from a midwestern city in the United States, Columbus, Ohio. One might ask, how did I experience 30+, mostly solo, ultra runs throughout Europe? I was fortunate enough to have worked for Klarna, an international bank based in Stockholm, Sweden, from 2014 through 2022. I never permanently moved to Europe, but I traveled extensively to the region, and took advantage of my time there to explore countries throughout the continent. I've also been a runner for 20 years, logging about 1,000 miles / 1600 kilometers a year, and have completed 30+ races in most ultra-distance running categories from 100 milers to 50ks.

Nearly every adventure in this book was accomplished over a weekend. My plan was to get to my destination late Friday or early Saturday morning, and then start my running without delay, so I'd have 9 to 12 hours for the run. I'd then overnight in a hotel, and on Sunday would either explore the city via running or complete my run if I still had miles / kilometers to go until my final destination. After I was done, I'd then head back to where I was working, primarily Stockholm and Berlin, late on Sunday or very early on Monday morning.

I'm thankful for my family, who put up with my long and countless absences from home. Their support and understanding have enabled me to pursue my passions. And I'm also thankful for my friend Koen who suggested the location of my first long run in Europe while I was visiting him for the weekend in Amsterdam. That run got me hooked on a quest to visit every country in Europe and explore it by running. Erik Dahl, an ultrarunner and graphic designer who I've known for years, also provided key guidance in the book's layout.

I hope this book inspires you to find your own adventure and use my experiences to help plan all or part of that adventure. Every run in this book is based on my personal experience and is ultra in some aspect, either by distance, elevation, or conditions. Always know your limits, research the run on your own to ensure you have got the most up-to-date information, and plan for the worst, but expect the best.

For more details on any run throughout this book, please reach me at
ultrarunningdestinations@gmail.com.

Luke Tuttle
Columbus, Ohio
April 24, 2023

TABLE OF CONTENTS

The United Kingdom and France

For most of my life, the thought of taking a picture at night, in the most northern part of Sweden, alone on a trail, would have been unthinkable. Until I was 44, the only countries in Europe that I'd visited were the United Kingdom and France. However, starting in 2014 when I began working in Stockholm, Sweden, I traveled to Europe frequently and visited nearly every country on the continent. I'm forever grateful for this opportunity, where I not only could explore and experience the incredible countryside, but also grow through my experiences from living and working in other countries, especially Sweden.

NORTHERN EUROPE

01 Denmark

02 Estonia

03 Iceland

04 Ireland

05 Latvia

06 Lithuania

07 Norway

08 Sweden

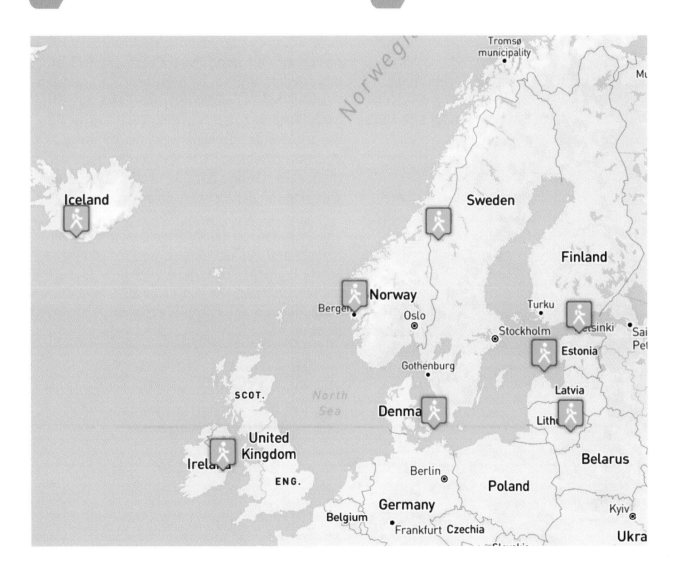

01

DENMARK
THE CHALK CLIFFS OF MØNS KLINT

Start	Liselund Ny Slot Hotel, Denmark
End	Liselund Ny Slot Hotel, Denmark
Distance	36 miles / 60 kilometers
Elevation	+1,700 feet / +500 meters

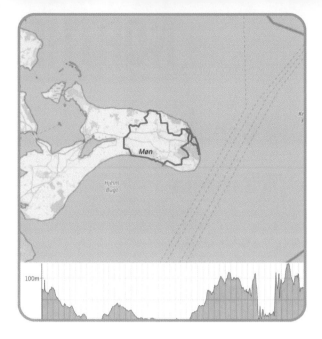

Getting There
I arrived in Copenhagen late on a Friday night, flying in from Stockholm, Sweden. I rented a car and drove to my hotel, the Liselund Ny Slot Hotel, less than two hours away.

Liked Most
The Møn Rundt trail offered a fantastic combination of rural roads, farms, rocky and sandy beaches. I enjoyed the beautiful scenery and variety of landscapes on my run. But I especially liked the unique cliffs at Møns Klint.

Unusual or Unique
Møns Klint's chalk cliffs and rocky beach made for a unique running experience. The area is also known for its "quality darkness," making it a great spot for stargazing.

Trail Description
The Møn Rundt trail provided a diverse and picturesque running experience. Starting my run, I traversed through charming farmlands with freshly harvested fields, creating geometric patterns that stretched across the landscape. The rural roads took me past traditional Danish farmhouses, grazing livestock, and vibrant green fields.

As I continued along the trail, I encountered a mix of rocky and sandy beaches that lined the Island of Møn's coastline. The north side of the island featured narrow, rocky beaches, while the south side had expansive, sandy shores. I alternated between running on the beaches and the tracks running parallel to them just inland, enjoying the distinct terrain and coastal views.

The trail also led me through patches of lush forests and quaint villages, further adding to the scenic beauty of the route. With little elevation gain throughout the run, I was able to maintain a steady pace and complete the course in good time.

While There
In addition to ultrarunning, Møns Klint offers excellent hiking opportunities, allowing you to explore the chalk cliffs up close.

Solitude

On these ultrarunning adventures, one aspect I enjoy the most is solitude. During my run along the Møn Rundt trail, as is often the case on these runs, I didn't see anyone else. This solitude makes the running even more special, as I'm fully immersed in the landscapes.

As I ran along the coastlines, through the picturesque farmlands, and eventually towards the bluffs overlooking the towering chalk cliffs, the sense of seclusion only deepened. The quiet expanse of the Island of Møn offered a unique opportunity to disconnect from urban centers I mainly worked in and embrace the peacefulness that nature provides.

02

ESTONIA
LAHEMAA AND KÕRVEMAA NATURE RESERVES

Start	Nõmmeveski, Estonia
End	Nelijärve Holiday Centre, Aegviidul
Distance	36 miles / 60 kilometers
Elevation	+1,700 feet / +500 meters

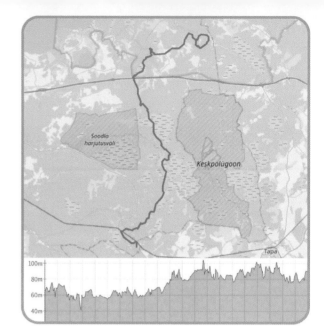

Getting There

I embarked on my journey to Estonia from Stockholm, where I was attending a work event. Excited for a quick trip before heading back to the US, I hopped on a mid-afternoon flight on a Saturday. Upon landing, I rented a car and set off for the village of Aegviidu, Estonia, where my hotel was located. The drive took around an hour, but due to a time-zone change, I lost an hour in the process.

Liked Most

What I enjoyed most about my Estonian adventure was the breathtaking natural beauty enhanced by the amazing weather that day. The clear blue skies, fluffy white clouds, and mild temperatures made for a perfect day on the trail. I was particularly struck by the serene areas in the bog where the sky reflected off the water, creating a mesmerizing mirror-like effect.

Unusual or Unique

While running through the Estonian forests, I was surprised to come across many families with large buckets, picking mushrooms. I learned that this is a popular pastime in the Nordic and Baltic countries.

Trail Description

This track is based on the Estonia Wilderness Marathon, with an additional 5 miles (8 kilometers) added to it. My chosen trail took me through two nature parks: Lahemaa National Park and the Kõrvemaa Nature Reserve. The route featured a mix of single track paths weaving through lush forests and stretches of wooden boards laid out across expansive bogs.

Throughout my run, I was constantly surprised by the variety of landscapes I encountered, from the dense forest paths to the open expanses of the bogs. The wooden boardwalks required a bit of extra caution, as one misstep could lead to a wet and potentially dangerous situation. I'd read that following into a bog can be dangerous due to how hard it is to get out. However, this added an exciting element to the run, as I had to stay focused and alert at all times.

While There

Because of my limited time on this trip, I didn't get to visit the capital of Estonia, Tallinn. However, I've heard from friends that the city is one of the most beautiful in Europe.

The Start

Many of the runs in this book involve being dropped off at the start of the trail and then running back to where I'm staying. It's daunting to watch the car drive off into the distance, leaving me alone in the middle of a remote place. But, it's also the most fun time, because this is when I need to focus on the task and get running.

There is also a significant moment of elation when you see a trail marker like this one in the picture to the left, showing you are on the right way!

03

ICELAND
FIMMVÖRÐUHÁLS TRAIL
SKÓGAR TO THÓRSMÖRK

Start	Hotel Skógafoss, Iceland
End	Hotel Skógafoss, Iceland
Distance	29 miles / 46 kilometers
Elevation	+6,736 feet / +2 053 meters

Getting There
Fly into Reykjavik Airport and rent a car. The drive to Hotel Skógafoss, where the trail starts, takes about 2 hours, and is much easier to do if you have your own transport.

Liked Most
Epic views of the interior of Iceland. From a single vantage point, one can appreciate the massive scale of Iceland prior to descending into Thórsmörk (Þórsmörk). One can see many waterfalls in the distance, large glaciers of many shapes and sizes, and a massive plateau that is the gateway to the lower valley below.

Unusual or Unique
Hiking near a volcano that relatively recently erupted. One of the cool sites along the snow fields worth a small detour is the highest point of the hike, the Magni Crater, caused by the Fimmvörðuháls eruption in 2010.

Trail Description
The trail starts out as a rocky road, but in many places, a trail in soft grass goes along the berm and the trail occasionally cuts across grass fields between the curves in the road. As you wind your way up the mountain, which is almost an unbroken climb to 3700 feet / 1127 meters, appreciate the views of the ocean to your back, green mountains to your side and snow-capped mountains in front of you. As you get higher up the mountain, the landscape becomes more volcanic. The amount of vegetation drops and snow drifts became common on the sides, but the trail remained dry. At the Baldvinsskáli Hut, you can take a break since there is a bathroom and a place to sit. Since I hiked this route in June, there was still a lot of snow, requiring many snowfields to be crossed.

While There
Make the short drive to the famous black beaches and the arch at Dyrhólaey. On the way back to the airport, find some time to relax at Blue Lagoon, a large open air pool heated with geothermal heating. Be sure to make a reservation as they get booked full since it's one of the most popular places in Iceland to visit.

Diverse Terrain

The interior of Iceland differs greatly from the slope of the mountain that comes up from the sea. It's always wonderful to be on a run where the terrain changes so much throughout the day.

Waterfalls

There are almost too many waterfalls to count on this run! At the start of the run, I stopped to take a photo of each one, but soon realized there were so many that it was better to just pause and take it in.

04

IRELAND
THE WICKLOW WAY

Start	Near Kyle Farmhouse B&B, Ireland
End	The Coach House - Roundwood, Ireland
Distance	32 miles / 51 kilometers
Elevation	+6,771 feet / +2 063 meters

Getting There
Fly into the Dublin, Ireland airport and rent a car. The drive to the B&B where we stayed is only about an hour from the airport. They drive on the left side of the road in Ireland, so if you are not used to that, spend some time on YouTube to familiarize yourself and have the mantra, "keep left, keep left", while you drive.

Liked Most
The challenge from the incredible change in weather between the peaks and valleys on the trail. It felt good to be so well prepared and have the layers to take on and off to keep me comfortable and safe the entire time.

Unusual or Unique
The extreme change in weather between the peaks and the valleys. Be sure to carry many layers of all-weather gear. It is likely you'll need it all.

Trail Description
The trail has a lot of variety from end to end. It started out with a rocky single track that transitioned to a dirt road / Jeep trail. There are cobblestone paths, rocky approaches to peaks, a soaked field where I jumped between puddles, a paved trail in a park, forest single track

and finally a few road sections. The landscape also has a lot of variety depending on the elevation and the remoteness of the particular section. On the taller peaks where I got above the treeline, the landscape becomes stark as the wind has scoured it. I had to take shelter behind the concrete monoliths to take pictures because of the high winds. I also passed farm fields with sheep and spent a good deal of time in forests. The run finished on streets, along hedgerows that led into the town with a friendly pub where I stopped.

While There
Hike up nearby Djouce mountain. Depending on when you make the trip, be prepared for a dramatic change in the weather between the base and the peak. At the peak it was near whiteout conditions.

Endurance

Psychobiology researcher Samuele Marcora defines endurance as "the struggle to continue against a mounting desire to stop". For me, the struggle to continue is balanced out by my passion to explore along with the feeling of accomplishment when I get to the top of a mountain, make it through a hard stretch, or finish my adventure.

05
LATVIA
THE SLĪTERE CIRCLE

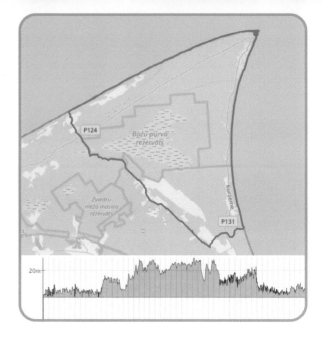

Start	Cape Kolka, Latvia
End	Cape Kolka, Latvia
Distance	31 miles / 50 kilometers
Elevation	+1,083 feet / +330 meters

Getting There
I began my Latvian adventure by landing at Riga, Latvia airport on a rainy Friday night and staying in a Soviet-era hotel in Jūrmala, a resort area only 30 minutes from the airport. The next morning, I drove two-hours north through the forest to reach Cape Kolka.

Liked Most
Running on the hard-packed beaches with the forest close to the shore, feeling disconnected from civilization, was a memorable experience. I also enjoyed crossing the bog on the forest trail, which felt like walking on a giant sponge surrounded by dense foliage.

Unusual or Unique
The remote beaches along the Latvian coast resulted from the Soviet occupation of the Baltic countries, which made these areas off-limits until 1991. On my run, I encountered a few campers, as well as participants of the Barefoot Baltic Ultramarathon, running in the opposite direction. I noticed a photographer taking a picture of me. The photo to the right is from that photographer. I found him online, emailed him, and he sent me the photo!

Trail Description
For the 50k Slītere Circle route I found, there was a mix of beach, forest road/trail, and additional beach. The forest trail led me through a bog and eventually to some farms, but it remained mostly a forested path or dirt/gravel road. The beaches offered great footing for running, and the last leg featured calmer waters of the Gulf of Riga. Be prepared for having soaked feet. The boggy areas in the forest, as well as portions of the beach where inlets of water had to be waded through, kept my feet wet the entire time.

While There
In Riga, I recommend visiting the Riga Central Market, admiring the Art nouveau architecture, taking a water taxi for a river tour, and visiting the Freedom Monument and Museum of the Occupation to understand Latvia's history. The city offers a variety of attractions that make it an excellent place to recover after an ultrarunning adventure.

Desolation

The desolation during these runs is often enhanced by items that seem discarded or run down. This boat, and some old tractors, added to the feeling during this run.

Isolation

It is sometimes strange how few people I encountered on these runs, even when passing by a farm or a town. While feelings of isolation can creep in, it's best to just push those aside and keep going.

06

LITHUANIA
NERIS RIVER AND
REGIONAL PARK

Start	Karmazinai, Lithuania
End	Vilnius, Lithuania
Distance	34 miles / 55 kilometers
Elevation	+2,647 feet / +807 meters

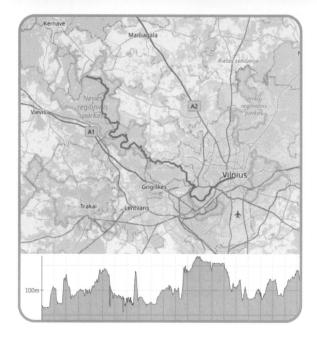

Getting There

My trip started when I landed at the Vilnius airport. Since I was planning to go on an ultra-running adventure, I had to find a place to stay along the track that roughly parallels the Neris River, about 30 miles / 50 kilometers west of Vilnius. I found The Guest House Slenyje, a bed-and-breakfast owned by a nice couple who offered to pick me up late on Friday when I landed.

Liked Most

The breathtaking views along the Neris River and the peacefulness of the surrounding dense forest were the highlights of my run. One thing I didn't like on this run was the sections with intense clouds of flies and mosquitos.

Unusual or Unique

The breakfast made up of fermented specialties by the owner of the B&B. On the drive there, I learned that the owner's wife was a well-known specialist in food fermentation, while he was an expert fly fisherman who runs tours attracting people from all over the world. Soon after I woke up, he brought over breakfast consisting of his wife's fermented specialties of homemade yogurt, sourdough pancakes, kombucha tea, and sourdough bread. It was probably the most unusual pre-run breakfast I've ever had.

Trail Description

Starting on a dirt road, the run changed to a riverside path, went through a thick forest, and occasionally shifted back to dirt roads. The trail featured some steep ascents and required a few detours through tall grasses on the shore. The run ended in Vilnius City Park, with a last stretch through the city. I wasn't able to follow my intended trail for two reasons. Some private homes had been built that forced me to run through tall grasses along the shore. Flies and mosquitoes also swarmed in several areas, forcing me farther inland where on dirt roads rather than singletrack trails.

While There

Visit Klanai Park and hike up to its famous three crosses. These three large white crosses are on a large hill set within a large quiet park with plenty of park benches to relax on along the river. The old town in Vilnius also has many nice places to eat. I particularly enjoyed a lunch outdoors in the sun prior to my flight out.

Unexpected Moments

I didn't expect to drink from this jug of water you can see on the left. But, I did. I started with 2 liters of water, but that wasn't near enough, and the trail didn't pass through any towns where I could buy water. Best I could tell on the map a detour to get water would have added at least 6 miles (10 kilometers) to the run. It smelled clean, and it looked clean, so I drank it. Don't forget a water filter!

I also didn't expect to see a pictogram about what would happen if you peed on that fence. Maybe it was put up because of construction workers on the road? I choose to increase my pace and get through that area quickly.

07
NORWAY
BERGEN NORWAY

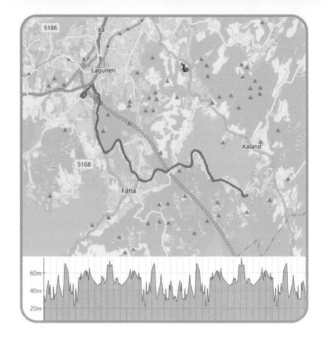

Start	Fanal Stadium, Radal, Norway
End	Fanal Stadium, Radal, Norway
Distance	26.2 miles / 44 kilometers
Elevation	+3,000 feet / +1 000 meters

Getting There
I flew from Stockholm, Sweden to Bergen, Norway with a connection through Oslo, Norway. However, if you are going in the summer, and have some extra time, I'd recommend you take the train from Oslo, Norway. I've heard from friends that it is one of the most scenic train rides in all of Europe. Once in Bergen, I rented a car since I wasn't sure about transportation options to the start of the marathon. For convenience, I stayed at the Clarion Bergen Airport Hotel, just a short drive from the airport.

Liked Most
Seeing Santa's House on the marathon course and also the very quiet run through nature.

Unusual or Unique
Given that they hold the race in December, in Norway, I assumed it'd be snow and ice, but I was wrong. The description on the marathon website says, "Welcome to Bergen – the City of Marathons and one of the most beautiful cities in the world. Bergen is "heaven on earth" for runners. Not too hot in the summer and a mild climate during the winter. Even in wintertime, the tracks are often free from snow and ice." There is very little snow in Bergen, but there is also a lot of rain. Bergen averages 239 days of rain a year, which is nearly 90 more days of rain than Seattle, Washington gets!

Trail Description
The marathon is an out-and-back on a rails-to-trails type course that is paved the entire way. The race starts and ends in a small stadium. It was a quiet affair without a lot of fanfare. The course is rarely flat, but with just gently rolling hills that add up to about 3000+ feet (1000m) of elevation gain.

While There
If you are here near Christmas, have the traditional Norwegian Christmas dinner, Pinnekjøtt. Pinnekjøtt is ribs from lamb that have been salted, and sometimes also smoked, to preserve them. It is a relatively easy meal to make, but it takes a lot of time to do it right. The meat is soaked in water to remove most of the salt, which can take around 30 hours. When served, it comes with a dish of melted fat you can pour over it for extra flavor. Absolutely amazing!

08

SWEDEN
JÄMTLAND TRIANGLE

Start	Storulvån Mountain Station
Overnight	Sylarna Mountain Station
End	Storulvån Mountain Station
Distance	29 miles / 47 kilometers
Elevation	+3,500 feet / +1 000 meters

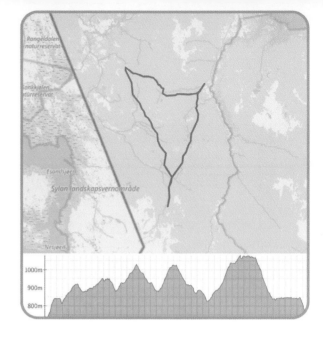

Getting There
My trip started with a one hour flight at 8am from Stockholm Arlanda Airport to the Åre Östersund Airport. I picked up a rental car, then drove two hours west to the Storulvån Mountain Station, getting there about noon. Of the three stations on this hike, Storulvån is the only one accessible by ground transportation. Make your reservations early at the STF (Swedish Tourist Association) website, as this is a popular hike. I ran to Sylarna, where I stayed overnight, as soon as I got there, and then stayed at Storulvånon the second night.

Liked Most
My quiet lunch at the Blåhammaren Mountain Station. I stopped in to have a beer, potato chips, and a chocolate bar for lunch after a cold 11 mile run from Sylarna Mountain Station. I had the place to myself since at midday most everyone is still out on the trails.

Unusual or Unique
The mountain stations operated by the STF must be some of the nicest in the world. These mountain stations are far more than just huts, they are proper lodges including saunas, sit-down meals, and a variety of accommodation options from bunk rooms to private rooms. Be-

sides these major mountain stations, there are also warming huts at the midpoint of each trail.

Trail Description
Overall, the trail was very runnable, but there was still a lot of snow on the ground, and large sections were through boggy areas with boards placed to keep your feet dry, which slowed my overall pace. The sections with boards can be very slippery when wet, so I took my time crossing them too. Stepping off a board in many places would have also resulted in a fall into water, which I wanted to avoid given the close to freezing temperatures. I was also careful crossing many of the snowfields, since they cover streams, which occasionally had holes in them where you could see the running water below.

While There
Have dinner at the mountain lodges, the food was excellent. Also, visit the impressive waterfalls, Handölsforsen and Tännforsen that are located nearby. Both have hiking trails that let you get up close to them and feel their power. For those who dare to brave it, there is even a suspension bridge that takes you directly above the Handölsforsen falls.

The Importance of Good Gear

This run was totally unexpected and only made possible by a sudden change to my work schedule. Fortunately for me, in central Stockholm, I could purchase this windproof and waterproof, yet breathable outfit. I also purchased a couple of fleece jackets so I could layer my clothes throughout the day. It's well worth the money to get high performance and durable gear since you depend on it to keep yourself comfortable and safe.

Storulvån Station

Sylarna Station

Blåhammaren Station

Warming Huts

09

SWEDEN
LIDINGÖLOPPETS COURSE

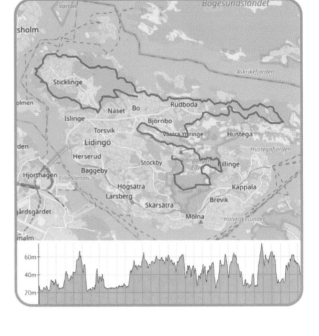

Start	Koltorps Gärde, Lidingö, Sweden
End	Grönsta parkering Lidingö, Sweden
Distance	18 miles / 30 kilometers
Elevation	+1,771 feet / +540 meters

Getting There

After working in Stockholm for over 5 years, I finally took a half day off and visited the nearby island of Lidingö to run the Lidingöloppet course. Public transit is available, but I opted for a quick 15-minute taxi ride from the city center to the starting point.

Liked Most

The Lidingöloppet course offered smooth forest trails with only a few short portions of road and paved pathways. I was impressed by the beautiful views of the water as the course dipped in and out of the coastline, showcasing excellent trail running just minutes away from a dense city center.

Unusual or Unique

The Lidingöloppet is the world's largest and longest cross-country event and is part of the prestigious Swedish Classic Circuit, which includes cross-country skiing, cycling, swimming, and cross-country running events.

Trail Description

Despite a couple of steep climbs, the course is very runnable and has over 2000 feet (600m) of elevation gain. The weather was perfect for running, with a light mist and temperatures just above freezing. The days may be short in November, but the course is well lit for nighttime runs. Lighting on trails is very common throughout Stockholm because the sun sets so early during winter.

While There

Stay at the boutique Miss Clara Hotel in Central Stockholm, which offers comfortable rooms, a fantastic restaurant, and attentive staff. Don't forget to try the pizza at 450 Gradi on Lidingö. It might be the best in Stockholm. If you're short on time, consider running one of the shorter distances on the Lidingöloppet course for a taste of what one of my friends describes as "pure Scandinavian bliss."

Traveling Light

On many of these trips, I would only take what fit into my Camelbak backpack since I needed to run from point to point with everything I needed for the weekend. Since I liked to go out in the city I was staying in, I'd also bring a set of merino wool clothes that were suitable to wear out to a nice dinner. Even with planning and having done it many times, there was something unsettling about heading for the airport with so few things. But, once at my destination, just having the bare minimum of what I needed felt liberating.

EASTERN EUROPE

10 Bulgaria

11 Czechia

12 Hungary

13 Poland

14 Romania

15 Slovakia

BULGARIA
RILA MOUNTAINS

Start	Belmeken Dam, Bulgaria
Overnight	Hotel Bor, Semkovo, Bulgaria
End	Kartala Ski Area, Bulgaria
Distance	49 miles / 79 kilometers
Elevation	+7,884 feet / +2 042 meters

Getting There

On my trip to Bulgaria, I left the logistics planning for Emil and Veneta at BgHike, who specialize in the Rila Mountains. I booked their Self-Guided Pack, which took care of planning the trail I'd run, hotel booking, and transfers. They picked me up Saturday morning from the Ibis Sofia Airport hotel and drove me to the starting point at the Belmeken Dam.

Liked Most

The beautiful mountain views and the well-planned route by BgHike were highlights of my trip. The remote alpine lake, the water fountains fed by mountain springs, and the Makedonia Hut were memorable stops along the way.

Unusual or Unique

Encountering semi-wild horses, shepherds tending their flocks, and abandoned buildings from dam construction projects were unique aspects of the trail. The encounters with Karakachan dogs protecting their flocks added an element of surprise and excitement. Karakachan dogs are an ancient livestock guardian breed native to Bulgaria. They are large, powerful, and well-adapted to the harsh mountain conditions of the Balkan Peninsula. These dogs have been used for centuries by shepherds to protect their

flocks from predators such as wolves, bears, and even human thieves.

Trail Description

The trail started at the Belmeken Dam and spanned 70+ kilometers over two days. It began with asphalt, but quickly turned onto a dirt road that made up most of the trail. Much of the trail was through dense forest, but there were also sections with sweeping views of the surrounding mountains. Other than the mountain shepherds, I'm not sure I saw anyone else these two days. Day one ended at Hotel Bor in Semkovo, and day two included an extremely steep section leading up to the Makedonia Hut, followed by a long downhill to the end. The run finished in the area of the Kartala Ski Resort.

While There

Exploring the Rila Mountains further is a must, with famous views like the Seven Rila Lakes and the Rila Monastery to incorporate into future runs.

Things Can Change in an Instant

As I came through this valley, I paused and thought to myself how amazingly idyllic this place is. It was a high point, and I was running with a smile on my face. However, in an instant, that feeling of euphoria turned to panic.

I heard the barking, and as I ran by the house, I saw a group of dogs staked to the ground, pulling at their chains, barking loudly.

One of them pulled their stake out of the ground and then chased me. About 20 minutes later, it finally turned back.

Unusual Sights

On long runs, you never know what you'll come across. Deep in a forest, I found a road crew asleep under their trucks, waiting for the next load of dirt to spread on the road.

There were also what appeared to be abandoned mini-dams as part of a water control system. These were fun to explore and imagine who it was that installed, then maintained them.

It's also not uncommon to come across spring water like this, but I rarely try it out since I cannot read the signs on them.

11

CZECHIA
SNĚŽKA MOUNTAIN

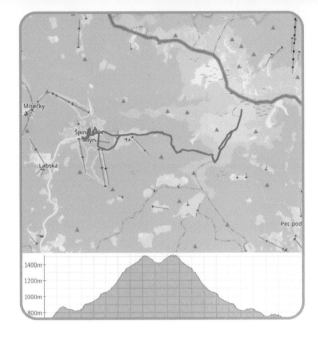

Start	Špindlerův Mlýn, Czechia
End	Špindlerův Mlýn, Czechia
Distance	13 miles / 21 kilometers
Elevation	+3,677 feet / +1 121 meters

Getting There

I set out from Wroclaw, Poland, in my rental car and took my time driving to Špindlerův Mlýn, visiting two tourist sites along the way: Project "RIESE" and The Grodno Castle. The drive included navigating the scenic "Hundred Curves Road" before reaching my destination.

Liked Most

The stunning views of the snow-covered mountains and the extensive network of trails around Špindlerův Mlýn make it an ideal ultrarunning destination. The town itself also offers a variety of hotels, making it a comfortable base for exploring the area.

Unusual or Unique

My initial goal was to run to Sněžka, the highest point in Czechia. However, the weather took an unexpected turn, with strong winds and freezing temperatures forcing me to reconsider my plans. Despite being an experienced runner, I found myself unprepared for the harsh conditions, which served as a reminder of the importance of proper planning and adaptability when tackling mountain trails.

Trail Description

Starting with a steep climb through the village, the trail then changed to snowy pathways. The trail to the peak was made up of packed snow that twisted through dense forest with several idyllic stream crossings on cut logs. The first part of the run was pleasant, but after cresting the first major ridge, I was hit with strong winds, snow, and freezing temperatures. Despite the challenging conditions, the landscape was breathtaking.

While There

Besides ultrarunning, Špindlerův Mlýn offers plenty of other outdoor activities, like hiking and skiing. The town also serves as a great base to explore nearby attractions, such as the highest point in the Czech Republic, Sněžka. Just make sure to dress appropriately for the weather and trail conditions!

Quickly Changing Conditions

As I began the run, there was no snow at the lower elevation, making for a comfortable start. However, as I ascended, the snow gradually increased, adding complexity and challenge to the run.

However, upon reaching the top, I was met with whiteout conditions that made it nearly impossible to see the path ahead. The harsh winds and heavy snowfall transformed the landscape into a disorienting and hostile environment.

The extreme weather served as a humbling reminder to plan for the worst, even during what started as a seemingly ordinary run.

12

HUNGARY
DANUBE-IPOLY
NATIONAL PARK

Start	Cave of Paul Valley, Hungary
End	Danubius Health Spa Resort, Hungary
Distance	26.5 miles / 45 kilometers
Elevation	+3,683 feet / +1 122 meters

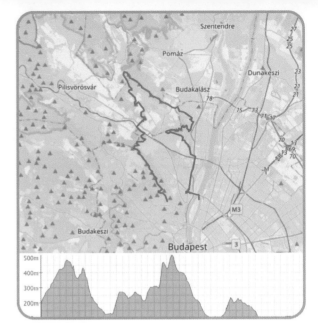

Getting There

One of the significant advantages of traveling within Europe is the abundance of low-cost and direct flights between major cities. I could have a full weekend in Budapest at a relatively low cost with my flight from Berlin, Germany. Upon arrival, I took a 40-minute taxi ride from the airport to Cave of the Paul Valley, the starting point of my run at the southern end of the park district.

Liked Most

My run took me through various terrains like road, paths, single track, and dense forest, offering a diverse and engaging experience. Notable highlights included the Guckler Károly Lookout Tower, which provided expansive views of the mountains and city, and the Egri vár másolata, a small medieval castle complex.

Unusual or Unique

The trail featured some unexpected landmarks, such as Teve-szikla, a natural rock formation and an old mine. The trails winding from the base up to the rim of the mine offered spectacular views of the city framed by the rock formations.

Trail Description

The run was a combination of road, paths through parks, single track and, in some areas, very dense forest and brush. I never knew what would come next on this trail. The run started on city streets, but then throughout the day the trail was a mix of forest and fields. The first milestone of the run after a steep climb is the Guckler Károly Lookout Tower, built atop an old World War II aircraft bunker. One of the best parts of the run was traversing a ridge that connected several peaks in the area because of the nice single track and elevation changes. The trail also offers some surprises, such as when it passes through Egri vár másolata, a small medieval castle complex.

While There

Besides running, there are many attractions to explore, such as the Roman City of Aquincum and museum, and Margaret Island with its running track. Budapest is also famous for its hot springs and hotels, like the Danubius Hotel and Spa Resort, which offers a relaxing experience after a day of running. The running track around the island it sits on is also great for a recovery run.

Views From the Top and Other Observations

One ascent on this trail was so steep it required a steel cable to help pull myself up. At the top, I was rewarded with a view of a village in the valley below. From here, the trail then runs along a ridge that traverses several of the peaks in the area.

I explored a small side trail and found a stone house built right into the side of the ridge that looked like it was built with stone quarried from right next to it. Who lived here, how long, and why?

On the last stretch along a portion of road, I passed the Roman City of Aquincum and museum.

13
POLAND
CZARNY GROŃ MOUNTAIN

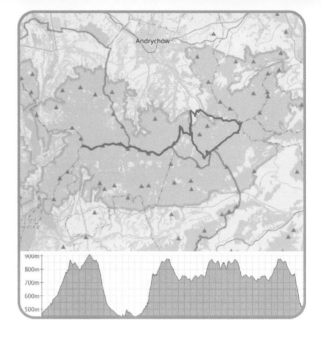

Start	Hotel & SPA Czarny Groń
End	Hotel & SPA Czarny Groń
Distance	27 miles / 44 kilometers
Elevation	+6,067 / +1 848 meters

Getting There
I worked in Wrocław, a city in Southern Poland. Known for its picturesque central square and international companies, Wrocław is only a 4-hour drive from Berlin. I used this city as a base for exploring the Southern Beskid Mountains, staying at the Hotel & SPA Czarny Groń in the Little Beskid Mountains, a 3-hour drive from Wrocław.

Liked Most
The Czarny Groń mountain provided an excellent starting point for my trail run, with the hotel at its base. The area is scenic and offers multiple trails that intersect at the peak of Laskowiec, the third highest peak in the Beskids.

Unusual or Unique
Visiting the Auschwitz concentration camp was a deeply moving experience. It's important to witness the evidence of such a tragic part of history to ensure it never happens again. The memorials dedicated to Pope John Paul II, who was from nearby Wadowice, were another unique aspect of this trip.

Trail Description
Exploring the trails in the Southern Beskid Mountains provided a variety of experiences, from wooded trails, to meadows, to rocky hill-sides. The dense forest sections provided a serene, shaded environment with the sounds of birds and rustling leaves accompanying my run. The open meadows allowed for stunning panoramic views of the surrounding mountains and valleys, showcasing the natural beauty of the region. As I navigated the rocky outcrops and steeper inclines, I appreciated the technical challenges they posed, requiring focus and agility. The variety in terrain and scenery throughout the trails kept each run engaging and refreshing, contributing to a truly memorable experience in the Southern Beskids.

While There
Besides trail running, I visited the Auschwitz concentration camp, enjoyed a relaxing evening at the hotel's spa and indoor pool, and explored the PGE Elektrownia Szczytowo-Pompowa / Pumped-storage Power Plant, which also has a small ski resort and amusement park.

14

ROMANIA
METRO AREA AND
VĂCĂREȘTI NATURE PARK

Start	Bucharest, Romania
End	Bucharest, Romania
Distance	35 miles / 57 kilometers
Elevation	+1,709 feet / 521 meters

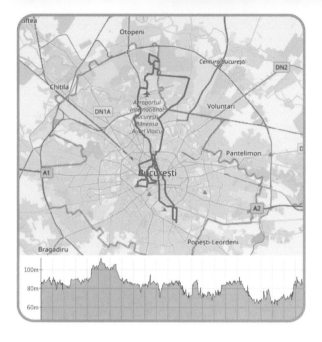

Getting There

I traveled to Bucharest, Romania, for an ultra-running adventure because of the affordable flights from Berlin on Ryanair. Though I initially knew little about the city, I discovered many interesting places to visit and planned a marathon course around them.

Liked Most

During my marathon run, I encountered fascinating sites like the Palace of Parliament, Romanian Athenaeum, Bucharest Old Town, and Văcărești Nature Park. I enjoyed running through these different urban and natural settings, offering a mix of experiences.

Unusual or Unique

I stumbled upon Văcărești Nature Park, a failed lake project started by Nicolae Ceaușescu. Over the years, nature reclaimed the area, turning it into a protected park teeming with diverse wildlife. The trails within the park made for a serene and exciting run. I also stayed at a hotel in the city center, where I enjoyed a conversation with the owner about his life and experiences during the 1989 revolution. He introduced me to Vișinată, a homemade cherry, sugar, and vodka drink.

Trail Description

My marathon route started in the heart of Bucharest, taking me through bustling city streets and past iconic landmarks such as the Palace of Parliament, the Romanian Athenaeum, and Bucharest Old Town. I enjoyed the energy of the urban environment as I navigated wide boulevards, like Boulevard Unirii, and the charming cobblestone streets of the Old Town. The city's sidewalks and walking paths made it easy to traverse the urban landscape. My route also included a forest park near the Bucharest Zoo.

In the Văcărești Nature Park, I followed a trail along the park's embankments, which encircle the area and were originally built for a failed lake project. Venturing inside the park, I discovered a diverse landscape of trees, high grasses, and many lakes. The peaceful and winding trails offered an excellent contrast to the earlier urban segments of my run. Along the way, I even encountered some of the park's wildlife, like a startled pheasant taking flight.

While There

Bucharest's many parks and urban oases offer opportunities for relaxation and exploration, making it an ideal destination for those seeking a balance between city life and nature.

Stumbling Into Awesome Runs

One joy of running is discovering unexpected places along the way. On the southern edge of the city, I stumbled upon a fascinating area hidden behind a tall fence. Intrigued, I found a break in the fence and followed the trail, which led me along the rim of an embankment reminiscent of a dam. After about a mile, I encountered a group of people, one of whom explained that the area at the bottom was a nature reserve filled with trails. Although the day was growing late, her enthusiasm for the area inspired me to return the next day for a longer run and take some more pictures. The experience highlighted the excitement of uncovering hidden gems during my runs, further fueling my passion for exploration.

Because of the tight schedule that weekend, I'd resigned myself to just running inside the city, but this unusual bit of nature turned it into one of my favorite trips.

15

SLOVAKIA
HIGH TATRA MOUNTAINS
ŠTRBSKÉ PLESO

Start	Penzión Pleso Hotel, Slovakia
End	Penzión Pleso Hotel, Slovakia
Distance	24 miles / 30 kilometers
Elevation	+6,000 feet / +1 800 meters

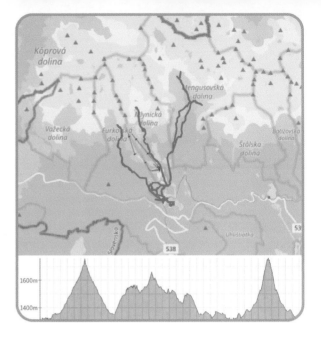

Getting There

I began my journey by flying into the Košice Airport in Slovakia. From there, I rented a car and drove to the highest village in the High Tatras, Štrbské Pleso, where I would explore the southern side of the Tatra Mountains.

Liked Most

The highlight of my trip was experiencing the Tatra Mountains in the winter, with its unique challenges like cold temperatures, snow, and high winds. Running across the frozen lake in the ski village was an exciting adventure.

Unusual or Unique

What made this trip a unique ultra-running destination was the combination of cold temperatures, elevation, snow-covered tracks, and high winds at the upper elevations. It pushed my limits as a runner and provided a challenging experience. It was so cold my water bottles froze while I was running.

Trail Description

I covered approximately 24 miles (30k) and 6000 feet (1800m) of elevation gain in two days, running on well-defined tracks that doubled as ski tracks. The lower tracks were suitable for running or fast hiking, but as I ventured further into the mountains, the snow got deeper and footprints were replaced by ski tracks. My Salomon Speedcross shoes with aggressive tread were essential for the snowy and icy terrain.

While There

Štrbské Pleso offers a charming ski village with a large lake, paths around it, and across the ice. The town has plenty of dining options, and the tracks are accessible right from the village.

Memorable Encounters

During one of my runs, I met a local who, surprisingly, was familiar with my hometown of Columbus, Ohio, despite never having been to the United States. It wasn't the first time I'd encountered this; he followed a European player on the Columbus Blue Jackets, a professional hockey team. As we talked, I realized I had become extremely cold from standing still for too long. To warm up, I had no choice but to say goodbye and run as fast as I could back to the hotel. It was a memorable encounter, reminding me of the connections we can make with others through shared interests, even in the most unexpected places.

Gateway to the Run

On this run on Germany's Westweg Trail, there was an actual gateway to the trail. Most times, though, there was a much less auspicious start. But whether there was a gateway like this, an old sign, or just a faint hint of a trail in the grass, the anticipation was just as great for what lay ahead.

WESTERN EUROPE

16 Austria

17 Belgium

18 France

19 Germany

23 Liechtenstein

24 Luxembourg

25 Netherlands

26 Switzerland

16
AUSTRIA
SCHWANBERG TO BORDER

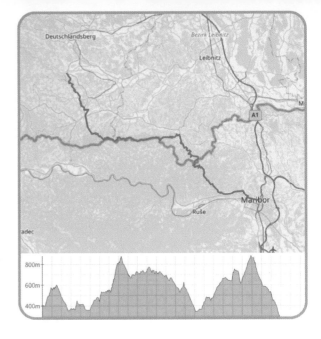

Start	Schwanberg, Austria
End	Maribor, Slovenia
Distance	44 miles / 70 kilometers
Elevation	+6,331 feet / 1930 meters

Getting There
I planned a weekend trip from Berlin, Germany to Maribor, Slovenia, flying into Graz, Austria, and staying at the Gasthof zum Flughafen hotel. On Saturday, I took a car service transfer from my hotel to Schwanberg, Austria, and began my run from Schwanberg to Maribor.

Liked Most
The trail passed through rolling hills with wineries and offered stunning vistas of the Austrian countryside. The solitude of the observation tower, Aussichtswarte Schlossberg, was a highlight.

Unusual or Unique
Running towards the border of Austria and Slovenia was an interesting experience, with the anticipation of crossing into another country, adding to the excitement of the run.

Trail Description
From Schwanberg, I started out on the Maria-zelleerweg 502 trail. It is a paved trail for a short while, then branches off into singletrack trails, crossing farms and through forests. The trail traversed rolling hills, some with wineries, made up of frequent vistas. I felt like I was making good time, so I stopped at a restaurant, Panora-maschenke Tertinek, in the town of Oberhaag, perched on the side of a hill overlooking the hills and valleys of Austria. From there, I headed north only a few miles and ran along the border of Austria and Slovenia. The main things to mark the border are white stone markers and a few small signs. However, a little later, crossing a road, I came across an old border checkpoint with the EU sign.

While There
Explore the beautiful trails and parks around Schwanberg, Austria. For wine enthusiasts, the region offers wine trails popular among bicycle riders.

Slow and Steady

I came across this snail steadily making its way across a quiet forest road. I doubt it could perceive the distance across the road, but something drew it to get to the other side. While I know the distance I've planned, I don't focus on it at all. It's better to just remain slow and steady, and live in the moment throughout the day. This way, you won't be frustrated by any missed turns, detours, or other unexpected happenings that lengthen the planned time and or distance.

17

BELGIUM
SONIA FOREST

Start	Hippodrome de Boitsfort, Belgium
End	Hippodrome de Boitsfort, Belgium
Distance	28.7 miles / 46 kilometers
Elevation	+2,000 feet / +610 meters

Getting There

During a visit to Amsterdam, I went on a day trip to the Ecotrail Brussels Trail Race in the Sonian Forest, just south of Brussels, Belgium. Borrowing my friend's car, I managed to drive the 2-hour distance from Amsterdam and still have time to enjoy the race and return by evening to have dinner with my friend in Amsterdam.

Liked Most

The Sonian Forest was an excellent place for an ultramarathon, given its proximity to Brussels. The run featured a forest canopy, rolling hills, and even some farmland.

Unusual or Unique

The Sonian Forest is a UNESCO World Heritage Site, and its proximity to Waterloo adds a historical aspect to the run. The track nearly reaches the Lion's Mound, which overlooks the battlefield where Napoleon was defeated in 1815.

Trail Description

The Sonian Forest provided a magnificent setting for the Ecotrail Brussels race. Runners had the opportunity to enjoy a variety of landscapes and terrains thanks to the wide network of trails in the forest. Most of the run took place under the lush forest canopy, with towering trees pro-

viding a serene, shaded environment.

The well-maintained trails consisted of packed dirt, leaf-covered paths, and occasional rocky sections, making the race both enjoyable and challenging for participants. The course was designed with a mix of gentle inclines and declines, as well as some steep, technical ascents and descents, which added an element of excitement to the run.

The course occasionally emerged from the forest into open farmland, offering stunning views of the surrounding Belgian countryside. The racecourse led runners through picturesque suburbs, showcasing the charming architectural styles of the region.

While There

If you're visiting Brussels for business or pleasure, be sure to explore the Sonian Forest's unpaved trails. If you happen to be there during the Ecotrail Brussels weekend, don't miss the opportunity to take part!

18
FRANCE
PARIS TRAILS

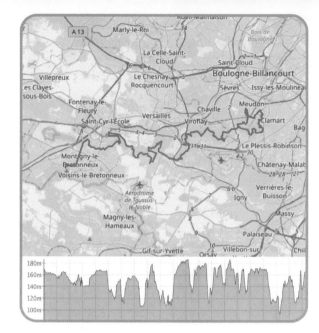

Start	Auberge du Manet Hotel, France
End	Ibis Paris Meudon Velizy Hotel, France
Distance	31 miles / 50 kilometers
Elevation	+2,994 feet / 912 meters

Getting There
My original plan was to run a loop course in the U.K., but because of the incoming hurricane Lorenzo, I was forced to make a last-minute change. I found a great flight to Paris, France from Stockholm, Sweden that enabled this weekend trip.

Liked Most
I was amazed at how remote the trail felt despite going right through a very urban area. The run consisted almost entirely of forest trails, with a mix of single track, forest roads, and dirt paths through parks and forests.

The high-point of the day was the Paris Observatory, where the grounds had manicured bushes and dramatic outdoor spaces. From one garden, I could see the Eiffel Tower in the distance.

Unusual or Unique
The most unusual event of the trip happened upon arrival in Paris when there was a massive explosion sound at the airport. The driver informed me it was likely just the bomb squad blowing up a piece of luggage, which turned out to be a common occurrence at Charles de Gaulle Airport.

Trail Description
I started out from my hotel on city streets. After about 3 kilometers of road, the trail entered the forest and continued through various parks and green spaces. The path alternated between dense woodlands and more open areas, offering glimpses of the city's urban landscape from time to time. The trail was mostly flat, making for a smooth and enjoyable run.

As I progressed through the route, I encountered several beautiful parks, such as Parc de Saint-Cloud, which offered stunning views of Paris. Along the way, there were a few small river crossings, adding some variety to the terrain. The serenity of the trail was surprising, given its proximity to the bustling city.

At the halfway point, I stopped at the Intermarché Super et Drive in Buc, France, for some water and snacks. This turned out to be the only time the trail emerged onto roads during the entire run.

While There
With proper planning, you can combine running and exploration, visiting central sights in Paris such as Versailles.

Sightseeing Along the Way

During my run through the urban trails of Paris, I encountered a surprise, a maze made of meticulously maintained hedges. Although I didn't venture into the maze itself, I couldn't help but marvel at the creativity and effort that went into crafting this living labyrinth.

Further along the route, I stumbled upon an ancient aqueduct. As I jogged along the trail, the ancient structure emerged from the trees, its arches towering above the path. It was a good reminder of the passage of time and the rich history of the region. These types of discoveries along the trail are often some of my most lasting memories of a run.

19
GERMANY
BERLIN WALL TRAIL

Day 1	Mauer Park to Frohnau S-Bahn
Day 2	Spandau to Heiligensee S-Bahn
Distance	28 miles / 46 kilometers
Elevation	+912 feet / +278 meters

Getting There

During my time in Berlin, I was staying on Bernauer Strasse, a street that once marked the path of the Berlin Wall. The Mauerweg (Wall Trail) caught my attention while researching a 100-mile (160 kilometers) race that follows the Berlin Wall's path. I decided to explore two sections of the trail over two days, taking advantage of the S-Bahn train stations as endpoints for my runs.

Liked Most

What I appreciated most about the Mauerweg trail was its blend of urban and natural environments. It is astounding to find such a long and diverse trail within a major city like Berlin. The convenience of having trains and taxis for point-to-point runs made the experience even better.

Unusual or Unique

The Mauerweg trail follows the path of the former Berlin Wall, making it a unique blend of history and nature. Along the trail, you'll find remnants of the wall, such as a preserved guard tower, which serves as a monument to the city's past.

Trail Description

The Mauerweg trail is a fantastic urban trail with diverse terrains and environments. One section takes you through dense urban areas and wooded trails, eventually leading to the Eichwerder Moorwiesen nature preserve. The second section begins in Spandau, following paths through dense forests, skirting farm fields, and eventually transitioning to a wide paved path along the Nieder Neuendorfer lake.

While There

Berlin is an excellent ultrarunning destination because of the accessibility of the Mauerweg trail from various parts of the city. You can choose from a variety of distances to suit your preferences, whether it's 20, 50, or 160 kilometers. Besides running, you can explore the city's rich history, culture, and culinary scene, making for an unforgettable experience.

20
GERMANY
BASTEI BRIDGE
SAXON SWITZERLAND PARK

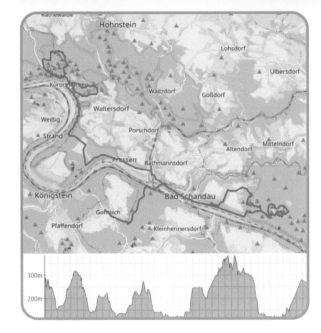

Start	Bastei Bridge, Germany
End	Gohrisch, Germany
Distance	26 miles / 42 kilometers
Elevation	+4,107 feet / 1 250 meters

Getting There

Before the pandemic lockdowns, I took a side trip on my way to Stuttgart for a robotics conference to go to the Saxon Switzerland National Park, east of Dresden, Germany. I rented a car in Berlin and drove to my hotel. I began my run by taking a cab from the hotel to the Bastei Bridge, an ideal starting point for this ultrarunning adventure.

Liked Most

The towering sandstone peaks of the park, along with the Bastei Bridge itself, were truly remarkable. The bridge allowed me to access fantastic views of the surrounding landscape.

Unusual or Unique

One unique aspect of the trail was running through the spa town of Bad Schandau. Despite being almost deserted because of the time of year, it was easy to imagine the town bustling during the summer months.

Trail Description

The trail began at the Bastei Bridge. From there, it meandered along the Elbe river, offering a picturesque running experience. The path led through rolling hills and lush green forests, with occasional clearings providing spectacular vis-

tas of the sandstone peaks.

Upon reaching the spa town of Bad Schandau, I ran through its charming streets, past historical buildings and quaint cafes. Leaving the town behind, the trail continued deeper into the heart of the national park.

The park's trails wound around the towering sandstone peaks, with some sections offering adventurous challenges, such as climbing ladders and navigating steep stairways. In some areas, I had to slow down to a hike in order to traverse the more technical parts of the trail safely. Along the way, I encountered unique rock formations, natural arches, and hidden caves, making the journey even more thrilling.

As I climbed higher, I was rewarded with breathtaking panoramic views of the park, the Elbe river, and the distant landscape. The sense of accomplishment after conquering challenging sections, combined with the awe-inspiring scenery, made this ultrarunning experience truly unforgettable.

While There

Take the time to tour the Bastei Bridge and spend some time in Bad Schandau.

Heights

Many of the trails in Europe involve trails that run along cliff faces, or have steep ascents or descents. Besides the heights on this run, there were also several large ladders helping to get onto the higher peaks in the area.

Once you get into the heart of the national park, you are free to explore the trails that wind into, around and up the sandstone peaks. There are many grand points where you can stop and take in the scenery. Some of these trails you have to hike, since they are up and down very large ladders and stairways. If you are afraid of heights or don't like open ladders, this part of the trip is one to avoid!

21

GERMANY
THURNINGEN FOREST

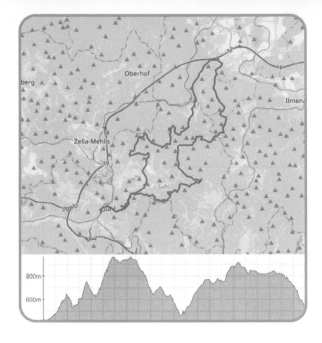

Start	Main Station, Suhl, Germany
End	Main Station, Suhl, Germany
Distance	35 miles / 56 kilometers
Elevation	+5,780 feet / +1 760 meters

Getting There

My journey began with a high-speed train ride from Berlin to Munich, taking advantage of the newly opened train line. I took an early morning train to Erfurt and made a quick connection to Suhl, where I would begin my 55k run through the Thuringia Forest.

Liked Most

The extensive trail network in the Thuringia Forest provided an excellent ultrarunning destination. The beauty of the forest, combined with the rolling hills and picturesque small towns, made the experience unforgettable.

Unusual or Unique

My run coincided with Ascension Day, which is also the German Father's Day. I had the chance to witness and take part in the unique festivities, such as drinking beer at mountain pubs, chasing a horse-drawn wagon filled with men listening to music and drinking beer and shots, and en-countering a woman with a "shot bandolier."

Trail Description

There are a ton of trails to run in this region, including portions of the Rennsteig Trail (including its highest point). So many trails, in fact, it was hard to choose where to go, but also made it easy to put together a 50k run (ended up being 35 miles / 56k) with 5700 feet (1700m) of elevation gain. I could make a nice loop consisting mainly of forest trails but with a few spots on quiet roads and through small towns. The small towns gave some insight into what East Germany was like as their infrastructure seemed to be less current, even as of now.

While There

Suhl, a small city in Thuringia, offers a variety of attractions and activities. Admire the baroque architecture of Ottilienkapelle or take a short trip to the Steinbach-Hallenberg Open-Air Museum. While in Suhl, don't forget to try traditional Thuringian dishes at local restaurants such as Thuringian bratwurst, potato dumplings, or Sauerbraten.

European Holidays

Little did I know Ascension Day is also the German Father's Day. Large groups of men known as Herrenentagspartie make their way to the nearest park/green space/whatever loaded down with beers and, paradoxically, on wheels. Whether it be a bike, beer bike, rollerblades, tractors, Boller-wagen(handcart) or even horse-drawn carriages, many men take a drunken day out. I could take part in the festivities by having a beer at a couple pubs on the mountain and also got poured shots of schnapps out of the back of a horse-drawn wagon filled with men that I chased up a hill. I also saw a woman with a "shot bandolier" hiking up the trail. These events made for a fun, not so serious day, with plenty of good people watching while covering a lot of ground.

Not the typical gear you see while out running

22

GERMANY
WESTWEG TRAIL

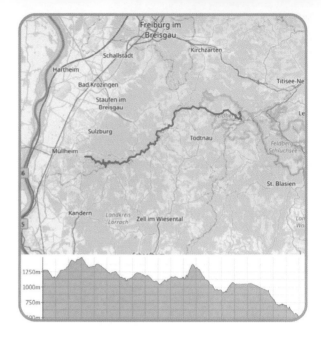

Start	Feldberg, Germany
End	Müllheim, Germany
Distance	33 miles / 53 kilometers
Elevation	+5,248 feet / +1 600 meters

Getting There

I was inspired by my German friends to embark on an ultrarunning adventure along the West-weg trail, a 285-kilometer path stretching from Pforzheim, Germany to Basel, Switzerland. My journey was organized with two major consider-ations: starting near Basel and Feldsee Lake, and concluding in Müllheim, the home of the pictur-esque Neuenfels Castle. I used a car service for efficient transfer between locations, although public transport may also be a viable option with more planning.

Liked Most

The fall colors throughout. The fall weather change further enhanced the beauty of the trail, as the vibrant colors of the trees create a mes-merizing backdrop for running.

Unusual or Unique

The trail's impressive length (over 285 kilome-ters) offers many opportunities for scenic runs and exploration.

Trail Description

The Westweg trail winds through Germany's picturesque Black Forest, providing breathtak-ing views and diverse landscapes. I was lucky enough to run this trail in the fall, so the color of the leaves was spectacular. There were long stretches of hard packed dirt with great views of the surrounding countryside. But there were also plenty of single track forest trails.

While There

Besides running, visitors can enjoy exploring the charming towns of Müllheim and Basel, as well as visiting the historic countryside castle, Neuenfels. The beautiful Feldsee Lake is a must-see attraction in the area. With so many sights to see and experiences to enjoy, the Westweg trail offers the perfect opportunity for an unforget-table ultrarunning weekend.

Exhaustion

While I was running through a deserted campground, the skies opened
up and a cold rain began to fall. After a long day on the trail, I was feeling exhausted and wanted to sit for a minute. Fortunately, I came across
a cabin and went inside to rest while I also checked my maps. I went into
that cabin exhausted, but knew I had to re-energize myself as I still had
a couple hours of running to get to my hotel. Since the sun was setting,
I was also motivated to pick up the pace to arrive before dark. The brief
stop enabled me to refocus myself, get past my exhaustion, and then
enjoy the beautiful misty forest that the rain left behind.

Day 2 Excursions

While I love the long distance point-to-point runs that make up most of this book, there is also great joy to be found exploring the area at the destination. In this case, it was a run to Castle Neuenfels. I went up early on a Sunday morning and had the entire place to myself. I had plenty of time to make this run before the car service picked me up and dropped me off in Basel.

23

LIECHTENSTEIN CROSS COUNTRY

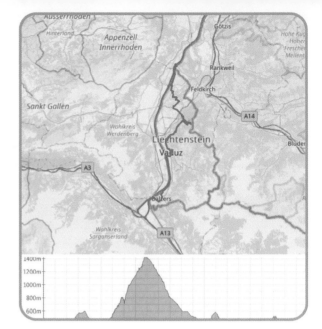

Start	Restaurant Löwenburg, Switzerland
Overnight	Vaduz, Liechentenstein
End	Sargans, Switzerland
Distance	39 miles / 63 kilometers
Elevation	+5,380 feet / +1 640 meters

Getting There

I began my cross-country run across Liechtenstein after a flight from Berlin to Zurich and an overnight stay in Zurich. The next morning, I took a train to Sargans, Switzerland, before taking a taxi to the northern part of Liechtenstein, where my run began near Restaurant Löwenburg.

Liked Most

Liechtenstein may be small in size, but it offers an immense variety of trails for running, from paved paths and grass trails to city streets and steep single tracks in the mountains. This diverse landscape makes it an exciting ultrarunning destination.

Unusual or Unique

The borders between Austria, Liechtenstein, and Switzerland are marked by small customs pavilions, but there are no restrictions or checks when crossing them. This allowed me to enter Liechtenstein with ease and begin my journey.

Trail Description

My two-day run took me from the Rhein River, through small towns, and into the mountains on Liechtenstein's eastern border. The trail consisted of well-maintained gravel roads and steep single tracks, with a rewarding stop at the Gafadura Hütte mountain hut. While sitting outside drinking my beer, I considered my options since I was thinking about going farther up to the peaks. However, the clouds were not clearing, and I read one should only attempt the route to Three Sisters if it is dry. So I finished my beer, then headed back down the mountain and on my way to Vaduz. The trails were very well marked, so it was easy to navigate a course. On the second day, I followed a more direct route along the Rhine River, visiting key sights like Vaduz Castle and Burg Gutenberg.

While There

Aside from running, I enjoyed dining at Löwen in downtown Vaduz, where I sampled locally produced wine. I also got my passport stamped at the Liechtenstein Visitor Center as a special memory of my trip. Great stops along the run are Vaduz Castle, St. Florin Cathedral, the Old Rhine Bridge, and Burg Gutenberg.

Crossing Borders in Europe

The journey began with me crossing the border from Switzerland into Liechtenstein, marking the start of the run. As long as you are within the Schengen area, there is free passage without the need to show your passport to a border guard.

As I made my way along the levee, the scenery transitioned into the stunning mountain range where the Three Sisters peaks are located. To celebrate reaching the top of the mountain, I took a break and enjoyed a well-deserved beer and some water.

The last image on the lower right captures the next morning as I ran along the river, crossed a bridge, and followed a train track, marking the conclusion of this long distance running experience.

24

LUXEMBOURG
ESCAPARDENNE LEE TRAIL

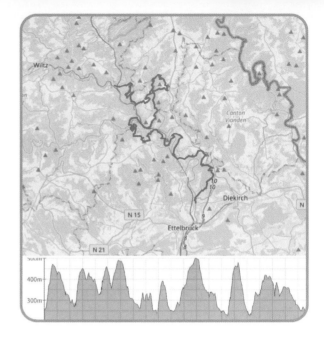

Start	Kautebaach, Luxembourg
End	Erpeldanged, Luxembourg
Distance	33 miles / 53 kilometers
Elevation	+6,624 feet / +2 109 meters

Getting There

My journey began with my flight landing in Luxembourg, where I explored Luxembourg City on foot, visiting the Casemates Du Bock, Adolphe Bridge, and Malakoff Tower. I then took a taxi to my hotel, Hotel Restaurant - DAHM, in Erpeldange, an hour north of the city.

Liked Most

The trail's breathtaking scenery, featuring sweeping valleys, pastures filled with cows, train tracks, and farmland, made it one of the most beautiful trails I've encountered. The remote, mostly single-track trail and forest roads provided a unique running experience.

Unusual or Unique

The Ardennes forest's impenetrability, which played a significant role in World War II, became apparent as I traversed the 31 mile / 53 kilometer Escapardenne Lee Trail, consisting of steep hills, rivers, and thick forests.

Trail Description

The trail started in Kautebaach, ascending a ridge that offered stunning views of the valley and countryside. From here, the trail was a nice mix of forest and open country trails. The trail also passed by the Hotel Dirbach Plage, which provided a convenient rest stop to refill my water bottles and enjoy a snack at the midpoint. The trail also included a steep climb up a mountain with para-gliding signs, leading to a fantastic viewpoint of a river in the valley

While There

During my stay, I explored Luxembourg City, visited historical sites, and enjoyed a delicious dinner at my hotel's garden. I'd recommend Luxembourg as an ultrarunning destination, as there are many other long-distance trails to explore in this beautiful country.

Aid Stations

When running an ultramarathon, I know where each aid station is located. Sometimes the race organizers even publicize what food and drinks they stocked the station with. On these journeys, I rarely knew what would be available when. But what is amazing is how often I come across a hotel or restaurant, such as Dirbach Plage, right when I need it. This restaurant is located right on the trail and they were nice enough to fill up my water bottles and sell me some chips.

25

NETHERLANDS COASTAL RUN

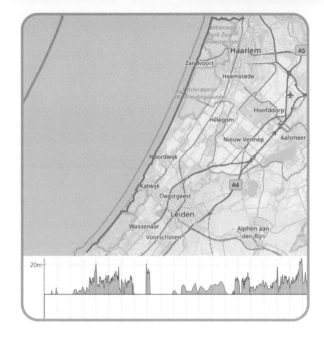

Start	The Hague, Netherlands
End	Santpoort-Noord, Netherlands
Distance	31 miles / 50 kilometers
Elevation	+965 feet / +294 meters

Getting There

My beach ultrarunning adventure in The Netherlands began with an early morning train ride from Amsterdam to The Hague. The 40-minute journey was just enough for a quick power nap before arriving at The Hague main train station. Once there, I spent some time finding a running store for supplies, and then made my way to the beach to start my run.

Liked Most

The weather was perfect for a beach run with blue skies and a gentle ocean breeze. The majority of this run was on well-packed sand, making it easy to run on. I enjoyed the solitude, as I had the beach mostly to myself, and the convenience of vendors selling water and snacks along the way.

Unusual or Unique

The most surprising aspect of the run was encountering several clusters of naked people on the beach. While it might not be unusual in Europe, as an American, it's not something I often come across.

Trail Description

My run started on the beach, where the sand was mostly packed and easy to run on. The journey ended with a right turn from the beach into Zuid-Kennemerland National Park. Moving from the beach to the nature park was a fast transition, and there were cows that are native to the region grazing the whole way. The track through the park extended almost all the way to the Santpoort-Noord train station.

While There

Take your time exploring everything that Amsterdam has to offer. The city is well known for its museums, food, and tours of the Heineken brewery.

26

SWITZERLAND
TWO SEASONS IN NENDAZ

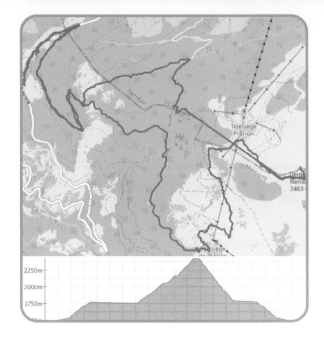

Start	Nendaz, Switzerland
End	Nendaz, Switzerland
Distance	12 miles / 20 kilometers
Elevation	+3,280 feet / +1 000 meters

Getting There

Nendaz, Switzerland, offers excellent running tracks for outdoor enthusiasts. The town is easily accessible by taking a two-hour train ride from Geneva to Sion, followed by a quick cab ride up the mountain.

Liked Most

The ability to run on both trails and ski slopes in Nendaz is a thrilling experience. Ascending to a peak with breathtaking views of the valley and mountains made the run even more enjoyable, while the steep downhill slopes presented an exciting challenge.

Unusual or Unique

Combining skiing and running during the same trip was a unique experience. I managed to sneak in a lunch run on the running tracks while on a skiing trip.

Trail Description

The trails in Nendaz offer a mix of terrains, from gentle running tracks to steep ski slopes. In the summer, you can run directly on the slopes which are mainly grass. There are also plenty of single track trails traversing the mountain, so all the trails are not as steep as a ski run. Prepared trails, that are relatively flat, circle part of the mountain and can be run on if there isn't too much snow cover.

While There

Nendaz is central to the 4 Vallées, the largest ski area in Switzerland. There are over 410 km of ski slopes to explore!

Ski Resort Running

European Ski Resorts are great locations for extreme runs throughout Europe. Unlike in the USA, there are even hiking tracks during ski season on the mountain, some even crossing the ski slopes. Several times while skiing, to my surprise, I saw someone hiking on the mountain.

Signs

The trail signs in Europe are very good. Whether they are very formal signs that are well maintained, or less formal signs such as this, most trails have signage at some point. That being said, for me, it was an absolute require-ment to have downloaded a full set of maps to my phone to aid my naviga-tion. The signs, while good, are not extensive enough, nor clear enough, to be your only form of navigation.

SOUTHERN EUROPE

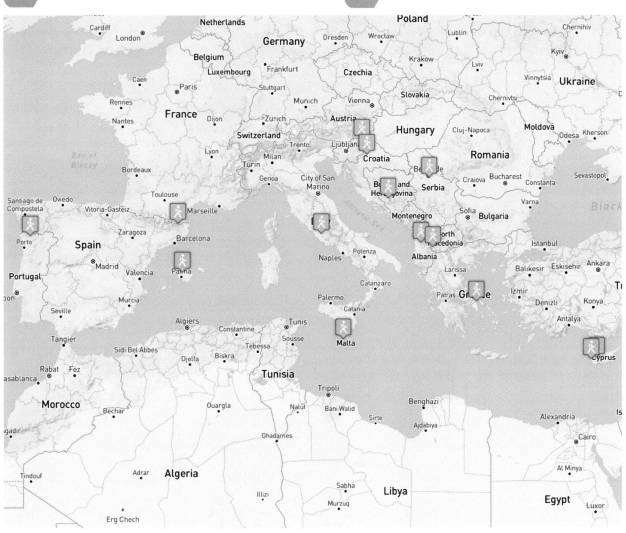

27

ALBANIA
DAJTI NATIONAL PARK

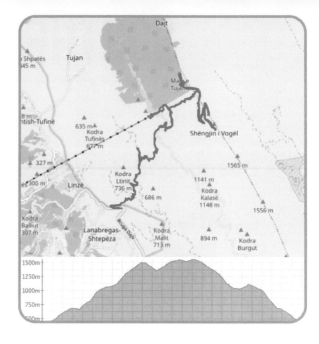

Start	Select Hill Resort, Albania
End	Select Hill Resort, Albania
Distance	14 miles / 23 kilometers
Elevation	+5,000 feet / +1 424 meters

Getting There

I flew into Tirana International Airport, and after a 30-minute taxi ride, checked into the Select Hill Resort Hotel. The hotel was conveniently next to a trail leading to Dajti Mountain and offered excellent amenities, including outdoor and indoor pools and great dining options.

Liked Most

The combination of rugged trail running with plenty of elevation gain on Day 1 and an 8-hour walking tour of downtown Tirana on Day 2 made this trip an exceptional experience. I enjoyed the contrast between outdoor adventure and city exploration.

Unusual or Unique

The presence of bunkers from the Cold War era, along with the potential sightings of snakes and brown bears, added an element of intrigue to the trail. The stunning views of Tirana and the surrounding mountains made the run particularly memorable.

Trail Description

Starting from a gravel road near the hotel, the trail transitioned from a rutted dirt road to a rocky and steep single-track. I climbed about 5000 feet / 1524 meters, reaching the top of Mount Dajti and Mount Tujanit. The Dajti Ridge Trail connects the two peaks, and there are several other trails to explore on the mountain. Near the very top of the mountain, the trail is mostly made up of jeep trail for the maintenance of the communication equipment.

While There

Besides trail running, I embarked on a walking tour of downtown Tirana, where I enjoyed traditional Albanian food. At the top of Mount Dajti, there is a cable car station with a café, a full-service restaurant, and a putt-putt course. Be prepared with cash, as the café doesn't accept credit cards.

Accessing the Inaccessible

A unique part of this run was all the cold war era buildings and signs that I came across. I'm not sure how long it's been since these areas have been opened up to the public, but it is apparent that for most of recent history this wouldn't have been a safe area to come. Running provides access to many areas not commonly visited for truly one of a kind experiences.

28
BOSNIA AND HERZEGOVINA
BLIDINJE NATURE PARK

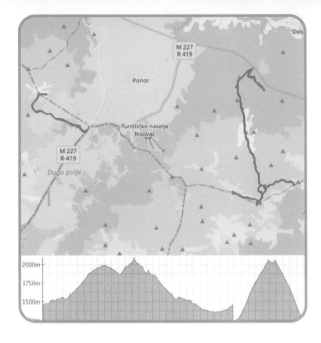

Start	Hajdučke Vrleti, Tomislavgrad
End	Hajdučke Vrleti, Tomislavgrad
Distance	23 miles / 38 kilometers
Elevation	+6,463 feet / +1 970 meters

Getting There
I flew into Split, Croatia, rented a car (although I would not recommend Avis because of excessive fees), and drove two hours to Blidinje Nature Park in Bosnia and Herzegovina. The drive was simple, with scenic winding roads and a straightforward border crossing at Kamensko.

Liked Most
Staying at the Hajdučke Vrleti hotel and restaurant was a great way to make this adventure comfortable and convenient. The staff was friendly; the food was excellent, and the location was central to several great hiking trails.

Unusual or Unique
The Blidinje Nature Park is an ideal ultrarunning destination, with many tracks that can be combined for 31 mile / 50 kilometer or longer runs. The Hajdučka Vrata, a stunning ring of stone, and Mount Pločno, the area's tallest peak, would make for an epic trail run.

Trail Description
The Vitlenica trail started in dense forest, opening up to breathtaking views of mountains and valleys. The hike included snowy sections and two highlights: the Hajdučka Vrata and the summit of Veliki Vilinac, which offered a spectacular 360-degree view of the surrounding mountains.

While There
Besides hiking, I enjoyed delicious meals at the Hajdučke Vrleti restaurant and observed people starting mountain bike rides from the hotel. The area is perfect for outdoor enthusiasts looking for a weekend of adventure and exploration in a lesser-known destination.

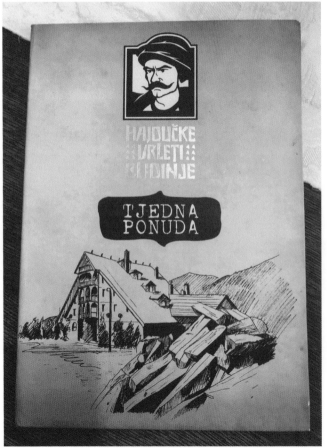

Choosing your Weekend Base

The location of a hotel is critical for an efficient ultrarunning weekend. I do not want to waste time with unnecessary transit. My hotel choices are also influenced by what restaurants were in the area. I would most often opt for the hotel restaurant since a restaurant dinner can also be the most efficient.

During my adventure in Bosnia and Herzegovina, I stayed at the hotel Hajdučke Vrleti. Not only was it the most convenient hotel in the area to the trails I wanted to run, but its unique design, and exceptional food, made it one of the most enjoyable stays I had during my European travels.

29

CROATIA
MEDVEDNICA MOUNTAIN

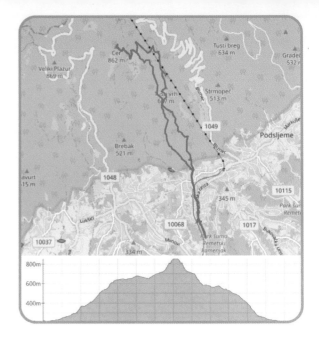

Start	Hotel Puntijar, Zagreb, Croatia
End	Hotel Puntijar, Zagreb, Croatia
Distance	9 miles / 14 kilometers
Elevation	+2,526 feet / +770 meters

Getting There

In Zagreb, Croatia, I stayed at Hotel Puntijar because of its proximity to the nature park on Medvednica Mountain, which provided many trails to explore. The location served as a perfect starting point for my two runs.

Liked Most

That I could run directly to nature from my hotel, but also be within minutes of downtown Zagreb where I got to have a nice dinner and tour the outdoor Christmas Markets.

Unusual or Unique

The snow-covered trees, weighed down by the heavy snowfall, created a tunnel-like trail, requiring me to snake my way above and below branches. It was an extraordinary experience, enhanced because I was the first to traverse the path that morning.

Trail Description

My first run took place on a snowy Saturday morning, creating an otherworldly experience as I made the first tracks through the thick, snow-covered forest. The untouched trail was challenging to follow but offered incredible views that I would have missed if I had waited for better conditions. On the second day, I embarked on a run to Medvedgrad Castle, high above Zagreb. The trail began in the forest and transitioned to a more heavily used path. The trail was on the upper edge of a steep valley, with a stream at the bottom. Despite icy conditions, I successfully made it to the top, where I enjoyed breathtaking views and explored the castle's exterior.

While There

During my stay, I visited the city center's Christmas markets, which offered great views because of the city's multi-level terrain. The markets featured stairways that allowed me to explore vertically.

30

CYPRUS
E4 LONG DISTANCE PATH

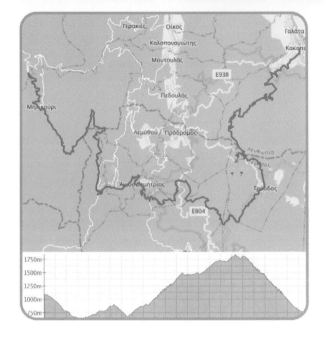

Start	Kykkos Monastery, Cyprus
End	The Mill Hotel, Kakopetria, Cyprus
Distance	38 miles / 61 kilometers
Elevation	+6,930 feet / +2 112 meters

Getting There

Over a long Easter weekend, I embarked on an ultrarunning adventure to Cyprus. The trip required over 8 hours of travel, including flying from Berlin, Germany to Larnaca, Cyprus, and driving to a mountain village. The island is easily accessible from various European cities, making it an ideal destination for an exotic ultra-run.

Liked Most

Cyprus' Troodos Mountains were a highlight, offering a breathtaking backdrop for my ultrarunning journey. The diverse landscape and picturesque scenery made for an unforgettable experience.

Unusual or Unique

One of the more unusual aspects of my run was the remoteness and solitude I experienced on the trail. I encountered very few people throughout the day, making it a peaceful and introspective experience.

Trail Description

The trail featured dense woods, ridge lines with ocean views, and rugged single track sections. Dirt road was very common throughout since much of the trail seemed to be access roads for heavy equipment. I was surprised to find a ski resort at the top of Mount Olympus, Cyprus' tallest mountain, with slopes still covered in snow.

While There

Cyprus offers a great mix of ultrarunning options with the E4 trail, coastal runs, and mountain routes. If you have more time, you can even enjoy a relaxing day on the beach after your run.

Taking a Break

Given the short duration of my trips, I was often under some time pressure to make it to a destination by a certain time. I would focus on keeping my pace up and only taking a break when necessary. However, looking back on these runs, some of the more memorable parts were a simple break where I'd eat some food and just take in the sounds of nature for a few extra minutes. Whether it was just wind in the trees, a gurgling creek, or the sound of a distant seashore, these moments were some of the best times I had.

31

CYPRUS
AVAKAS GORGE

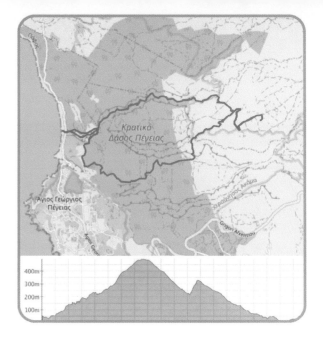

Start	Avakas Gorge Parking, Cyprus
End	Avakas Gorge Parking, Cyprus
Distance	13 miles / 21 kilometers
Elevation	+2,272 feet / +693 meters

Getting There

By pure chance, I saw on Facebook that my cousin would be in Cyprus at the same time I'd be there. I decided to visit him and his family in Paphos, Cyprus, while I was in the country. The 60 mile / 100 kilometer drive from Kakopetria provided an opportunity to explore the winding mountain roads and get a sense of the land-scape before my long run on a Sunday morning.

Liked Most

The drive itself was a scenic adventure, show-casing the beautiful nature and diverse land-scapes of Cyprus. Catching up with my cousin and his family after eight years was also a won-derful experience.

Unusual or Unique

Running through the Avakas Gorge, I found the trail to be a mix of narrow passages with vertical rock faces and wider sections with dense vege-tation. The many stream crossings and challeng-ing terrain made for an exciting run.

Trail Description

Starting at the gorge, the trail followed a stream and required many crossings. After exiting the gorge, I ran up to a plateau for panoramic views and created a loop by connecting two trails not linked on my GPS map, using goat paths as a guide. These paths climbed to some farmland where there was an excellent view of the valley the gorge sat in, as well as the ocean.

While There

In addition to the Avakas Gorge hike and run, visitors can explore the coastal town of Paphos, visit the Paphos Castle, and take in the beauti-ful ocean views. The diverse landscape offers countless opportunities for outdoor enthusiasts to enjoy hikes, runs, and sightseeing.

Going Beyond the Beaten Track

Nearly everyone who visits the Avakas Gorge would either hike it one way and take a bus back, or just hike in and hike out. While it is an amazing place to experience, if you continue well past it up the mountain, you get to see the gorge from a much different context. In addition, while the gorge can be busy, I didn't see anyone else in the mountain trails over-looking it. Take some time to seek these side trips. They can often be the most scenic and rewarding.

32

GREECE
THE AUTHENTIC MARATHON

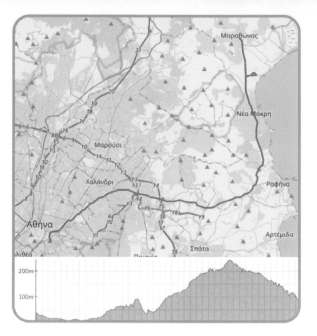

Start	Marathon, Greece
End	Panathenaic Stadium, Athens, Greece
Distance	26.2 miles / 42 kilometers
Elevation	+1,791 feet / +546 meters

Getting There

Athens is easily accessible with many direct flights from various European cities. I was fortunate enough for my travel schedule to align with the Athens Authentic Marathon, allowing me to take part in the event.

Liked Most

The atmosphere of the Athens Authentic Marathon was friendly, and the finish at the Panathenaic Stadium was an amazing experience. Running the "real" marathon route was an unforgettable opportunity.

Unusual or Unique

The starting point of the marathon was the most unusual one I've ever experienced, with people huddled in corners trying to keep warm and others running circles on the track at the Marathon Municipal Stadium.

Trail Description

The marathon course was traditional in that it consisted of city streets the entire way. The course wound through several small villages where many people came out to cheer. I didn't feel bored at any point as I do in some marathons. The variety of buildings, historic sites, and the friendly people kept my interest the entire time.

Aside from the marathon, Athens has an extensive trail network in a large park. The trails offer elevation changes and breathtaking views of the surrounding ocean and towns. These trails are perfect for exploring the city on foot.

While There

Athens is a great city to explore historical sites, such as the Acropolis, and hike up Mount Lycabettus for a drink while watching the sunset.

33
ITALY
VIA FRANCIGENA TRAIL

Start	Frascati, Italy
End	Pantheon, Rome, Italy
Distance	33 miles / 55 kilometers
Elevation	+3,500 feet / +1 000 meters

Getting There

I took a round trip flight from Berlin, Schönefeld Airport to Ciampino Airport. The flight times on Ryanair were perfect for a weekend trip. I landed at 8:30am Saturday and returned at 9:00pm on Sunday evening. At the time of this trip, Uber worked in Rome, so it was super easy to get to Frascati, Italy, where the trail starts, for only 32 EUR.

Liked Most

The diversity of the run. The trail is made up of forest trails, fields, old Roman roads, a trail that overlooked a large lake, and a small village that also overlooked the lake, with ancient sites and artifacts that kept the run interesting.

Unusual or Unique

The run was along the Via Francigena trail, an old pilgrimage trail that people have taken to Rome for 100s of years, with parts of the trail alongside walls that seemed to have bordered some old regal or royal properties. There are many ancient sights to see along the way.

Trail Description

The trail starts at the edge of the Parco dei Castelli Romani Park, that is southeast of Rome, Italy. The plan for the day was to run through the park then link up with the Via Francigena trail. It's an old pilgrimage trail that people have taken to Rome for 100s of years and has a lot of history and artifacts along the way. Much of the run was along old Roman roads that were "paved" with large cobblestones with rolling hills that added up to about 3500 feet (1000m) of elevation gain over the 33 miles (55k). The second half of the run was completely flat along the Via Francigena trail. The run wrapped up by passing The Colosseum and then finishing at the Relais Maddalena hotel in a quaint square next to the Pantheon.

While There

Visit Vatican City and go to the top of St Peter's Basilica Dome (551 steps). From this vantage point, you can look out over the city and see the mountain ranges far off in the distance where this trail run started.

Trailheads

Trailheads are not very awe-inspiring in nearly every case. Maybe there is a sign, maybe not. But what makes trailheads special in Europe is that they are entryways to amazing journeys, and very often they are just a taxi ride from an airport.

Trail Ends

The end of a trail is both a triumph and a letdown. A triumph because you made it, but also a letdown because the journey is over. In Europe, the trail end is often a nice hotel or monument in the city, well positioned for a second day of touring.

34

MALTA
GOZO COASTAL TRAIL

Start	Ghonga Bus Stop Xagħra, Malta
End	Ghonga Bus Stop Xagħra, Malta
Distance	31 miles / 50 kilometers
Elevation	+5,000 feet / +1 500 meters

Getting There
I took a flight from Stockholm to Malta with a layover, as there were no direct connections. Malta is the most southern EU member country, so it takes some extra time to get there from northern Europe. I rented a car and then took the ferry to reach Gozo, the northern island of Malta. The ferry ride took about 2.5 hours, but it offered a great view of the cliffs along the coastline.

Liked Most
The lasting impression I have of Malta is running the trails along the high cliffs above the ocean. The island offers breathtaking views, such as the Wied il-Mielaħ Window.

Unusual or Unique
Malta is known for its caves and natural rock formations. These naturally carved bridges, as well as sheer cliffs, kept the run interesting at all times.

Trail Description
The trail around Gozo took me along high cliffs, through rugged trails, and past beautiful inlets carved by the ocean. The inlets where the ocean carved out deep recesses into the island were among the highlights of the trail. I'd put the running experience up there with other iconic runs such as a traverse of the Grand Canyon. The island's trails feature many types, with some just a few feet from a sheer drop-off to the ocean, and over 5000 feet (1500m) of elevation change during the 50k run. My 50k run ended on a village street heading to the hotel after pushing through dense underbrush and roads in the last miles.

While There
Explore the island's caves, try local cuisine like the food at Tal Furnar, and take in the natural beauty of the rock formations and ocean views. If you have the time, the main island of Malta is much more commercial and offers many other activities beyond those that are on Gozo.

Coastal Trails

Running on coastal trails offers a unique blend of natural beauty, challenging terrain, and an ever-changing landscape. Ocean breeze accompanied by the sound of waves crashing against the shore is nature's mantra to help keep you going on a long run.

My ultrarun in Gozo perfectly encapsulated the essence of coastal trail running. The 50k trail around the island presented me with views of the ocean, cliffs, and diverse landscapes. Initially skeptical because the road from the hotel to the sea wasn't very scenic, I was soon captivated by the high cliffs, elevation changes, and various trail types I encountered during my run. I enjoyed navigating trails just a few feet from a sheer drop off to the ocean.

35

NORTH MACEDONIA
GALICICA NATIONAL PARK

Start	Peshtania, North Macedonia
End	Ohrid, North Macedonia
Distance	18 miles / 29 kilometers
Elevation	+5,174 feet / +1 577 meters

Getting There
Ohrid St. Paul the Apostle Airport hosts occasional direct flights, such as the early one I caught with TUI Airlines from Amsterdam. The proximity of the airport to the town—only a 20-minute drive—means you'll be exploring Ohrid soon after landing.

Liked Most
Ohrid boasts a perfect mix for the ultrarunner: proximity of intense trails to the town, the inviting, clear lake for post-run relaxation, and a picturesque town enriched with history, delightful cuisine, and unparalleled views. These characteristics, combined with its recognition as a UNESCO World Heritage Site, make Ohrid an unbeatable ultrarunning destination.

Unusual or Unique
During my run, I encountered an unexpected challenge that stood out: a swarm of bees and unusually large horse flies. These relentless companions buzzed around me for most of the run. Even the briefest stops would have them landing on me.

Trail Description
I chose the 40k route from the options provided by the Ohrid Ultra-Trail race, which meandered through Galicica National Park. Beginning at Peshtani, a lakeside village, the trail sharply ascends, gaining 3600 feet (1100m) in the initial 4.5 miles (7 km). This intense climb offered glimpses of the lake and a mix of dense vegetation and challenging terrains.

As I approached Chumo Vlaga peak, the path became less defined, with dense foliage making the trail hard to follow. The unusual rainfall that year had led to more grass and plant growth than usual, including a memorable stretch through stinging nettles. Although there was no denying the beauty of the trail, the real highlight was the views of Lake Ohrid and Lake Prespa from certain vantage points. The diverse settings, from dense forests to ridge trails, were always engaging. Still, due to unclear trail markings, a reliable mapping app, like Gaia GPS, is a requirement.

While There
Spend time relaxing at the serene Monastery of Saint Naum and along the pristine shores of Lake Ohrid. The lake, with its crystal-clear waters fed by springs flowing through the monastery grounds, is the perfect backdrop for relaxation. The local cuisine is also excellent, especially the local fish from the lake.

Unexpected Challenges

I didn't expect to be so challenged by this trail, and it ended up being one of the toughest runs I've done anywhere. There were stretches where the trail disappeared due to lack of maintenance, but also because the grass and other plants grew so tall from the unusual amount of rain this year. Despite being really focused on my GPS track, an inconspicuous fallen sign on the ground grabbed my attention. I then fell for that classic trail runner's pitfall, getting sidetracked and missing the right trail turn because I was looking the wrong way.

In addition, the local bees and horse flies kept me from stopping for even a moment. They were so thick, one even photo bombed my selfie. And finally, the intense sun, high temperatures, and the 3600 feet (1100 meters) of elevation gain in the first 4.5 miles (7 km) made for a very physical challenge too.

36

PORTUGAL
PENEDA-GERÊS
NATIONAL PARK

Day 1	Vilar da Veiga, Portugal
Day 2	Rio Caldo, Portugal
Distance	19 miles / 30 kilometers
Elevation	+6,000 feet / +1 829 meters

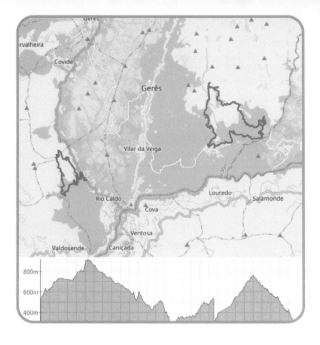

Getting There
I found a low-cost round trip flight from Berlin to Porto, Portugal, for only $135. After arriving late at night, I stayed at a Comfort Inn just outside the airport. The next morning I drove about an hour to the national park where my run started. I just parked my car and took off on the trail.

Liked Most
The amazing waterfalls, lush landscape in January, granite buildings, small villages, and old cart paths made the national park a memorable and picturesque running location.

Unusual or Unique
The surprisingly green landscape and many waterfalls in January set this location apart.

Trail Description
I did two runs while in the area. The PR 14 route took me past waterfalls, granite buildings, and small villages, with old cart paths to navigate. The run had a good elevation gain, and a cold rain made it challenging because the granite and rocks across streams were very slick. Most of the tracks were composed of dirt roads.
On the second day, I took the PR 7 route. This route was interesting because it went through an area that suffered extensive fire damage. The trail was likely bulldozed to provide access to fire vehicles, but there was also a good bit of erosion because of the lack of ground coverage.

While There
Staying at the Pousada Geres-Caniçada hotel offered an amazing view over the valley and a cozy fireplace to relax after the run. The welcoming staff and great food made it a very enjoyable place to relax after my runs.

Secret Areas

Sometimes an area seems like it's a well kept secret so that only a few chosen people can experience it. This valley I came across is one such example. The stream, the colors of the foliage, and the lightly traveled path added up to a very special experience. There is no way to predict when you will see something like this on a long run, but when you do, it's important to live in the moment and experience it to your fullest.

37

SERBIA
AVALA TOWER TO BELGRADE FORTRESS

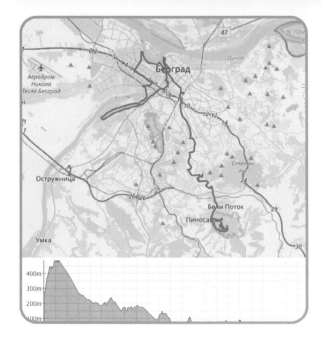

Start	Avala Tower, Belgrade, Serbia
End	Belgrade Fortress, Serbia
Distance	35 miles / 57 kilometers
Elevation	+3,038 feet / +926 meters

Getting There

After arriving at Belgrade Airport, I made my way to a very busy taxi waiting area. I planned to use Taxify (now Bolt) for transportation, but faced difficulties finding a cab and also discovered in-app payment wasn't available. In the end, I chose a taxi with a set price. I recommend pre-booking your ride when starting your run straight from an airport to avoid wasting time like I did trying to figure out the options.

Liked Most

The variety of urban and rural landscapes made for interesting runs both within the city and outside of it. I enjoyed the views of the Avala Tower, Belgrade Fortress, and the Ada Bridge, as well as running through Memorial Park Jajinci and around Lake Sava.

Unusual or Unique

Belgrade offers a chance to experience history firsthand, from the remains of the NATO attacks in 1999 to World War II memorials. The Aeronautical Museum Belgrade has a unique collection of aircraft, including the wreckage of American fighter planes shot down during the war in 1999.

Trail Description

My first run began at Avala mountain, through urban areas with limited running space, and finished in the city center. The run was mostly on city streets with a few areas going off onto trails. On the second day, I ran a 16-mile (26k) route along the rivers, parks, and lakes, enjoying the Ada Bridge and Lake Sava.

While There

I had dinner at Ambar on the Sava River waterfront and stopped at a café near Lake Sava to enjoy the sun. Belgrade offers many historical sites, museums, and opportunities for exploration both within the city and in the surrounding countryside.

38

SLOVENIA
BORDER TO MARIBOR

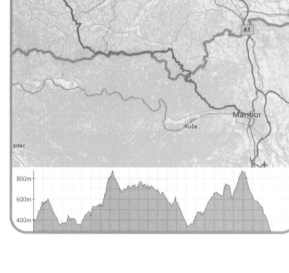

Start	Schwanberg, Austria
End	Maribor, Slovenia
Distance	44 miles / 70 kilometers
Elevation	+6,331 feet / +1 930 meters

Getting There
I planned a weekend trip from Berlin, Germany to Maribor, Slovenia, flying into Graz, Austria, and staying at the Gasthof zum Flughafen hotel. On Saturday, I took a car service transfer from the hotel to Schwanberg, Austria, and began my run from Schwanberg to Maribor.

Liked Most
The trail offered picturesque views of rolling hills, valleys, and wineries in both Austria and Slovenia. I enjoyed stopping at the Panoramaschenke Tertinek restaurant in Oberhaag, Austria, and the Aussichtswarte Schlossberg observation tower.

Unusual or Unique
Running across the open border between Austria and Slovenia and the hops farms.

Trail Description
I entered Slovenia by foot from Austria (See the Austrian run in this book). I continued on and crossed wineries nestled in the valleys, and also past the first hops farms I've seen. Slovenia is apparently famous for hops. The trails in Slovenia were more remote, with fewer houses than in Austria. It was getting later in the day, but the route I had drawn was keeping to roads in this

section and I wanted to do more trail. Seeing a trail on my Gaia GPS map, I detoured off the road and into the forest. This turned out to be one of the toughest sections, so it cost me a lot of time.

I got past this difficult section, then kept moving towards my goal of Maribor. Problem was, the trail I'd mapped out came across a private road marked as "Neighbor's Only". In the beginning, I thought it was probably alright to go down the wide dirt road, but after a short time, it became narrower and curved, which made me feel uncomfortable. I retraced my steps and studied the map to find an alternate route that connected with one of the main trails. I found a way, but I'd still need to cross an area that looked strange on the map, as it looked more like a maze. I suspect this is a hunting area with groomed paths for the animals to follow, but it was super weird to traverse, so I got through as fast as I could.

While There
After the run, I enjoyed a recovery walk through Maribor, exploring trails and parks north of the city. Slovenia offers beautiful long-distance trails and wine trails popular with cyclists.

Explore nearby...

 Explore   Driving   Transit

When Things Do Not Go According to Plan

This is the moment where I realized I still had about 12 miles (20 km) to get to my hotel in central Maribor. Besides that, the sun was setting and a cold rain started to come down. I had originally planned a 31 mile (50 km) run, but I clearly had miscalculated. I came across a covered park bench outside of a mountain tavern so I stopped and let the rain pass and changed into dry clothes and put on my rain jacket and pants. This is exactly why I always bring my rain/wind/cold gear because you never know what will happen weather wise, especially in a mountainous area. I wasn't really looking forward to another two hours of running, but it was what I needed to do. The last couple hours of running were in the dark, especially when in the dense forest, but a full moon lit the sky once I got onto the main road that followed the Drava River into Maribor. The trail was wide and easy to navigate by a flashlight, so it never felt unsafe. Except for one section, with lots of barking dogs, that thankfully were behind a tall fence.

39

SPAIN
MOLLÓ TRAIL ULTRAMARATHON

Start	Molló, Spain
End	Molló, Spain
Distance	27 miles / 43 kilometers
Elevation	+9,980 feet / +3 044 meters

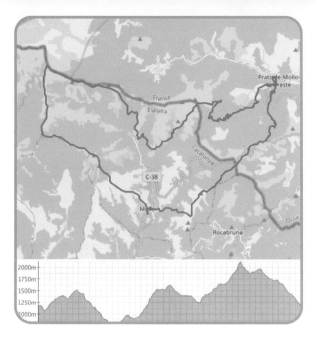

Getting There

I began my journey by flying into Barcelona, Spain, renting a car, and driving two hours north to Molló. Be sure to take your time on the drive, as there are several cities to stop and tour along the way. Molló is a small, picturesque town with a single narrow city street, residences, and small shops.

Liked Most

Taking part in the Molló Trail Ultramarathon was an unforgettable experience. The course is a loop starting and ending in Molló and features excellent single track, cattle trails, and dirt/gravel roads. The race winds through small towns and showcases the stunning Pyrenees Mountains.

Unusual or Unique

A language barrier was present, as most people in the area spoke French, Spanish, or Catalan, but not English. The eating customs were different too, with dinner typically eaten late in the evening. Additionally, I was surprised by the sprint start at the beginning of the ultramarathon, which is uncommon in the US.

Trail Description

The racecourse was diverse, passing through mountain trails, high pastures, and several small towns. The first couple miles are a very narrow single track where there is no passing possible. You'll find amazing single track, cattle trails and dirt/gravel roads on the course. The trail winds through a few small towns too, breaking up the scenery. One town being especially unique because I don't think I've ever seen a road so steep. The slippery street was very tough to get up because of the rain. A particularly memorable moment was crossing the ridge-line of several mountains during a storm, experiencing high winds, hail, and sunlight simultaneously.

While There

Exploring the towns along the drive from Barcelona to Molló is highly recommended, as each has a large church, town square, open-air markets, and cafes. The Calitxo Hotel is an excellent choice for your stay in Molló. Even if you're not taking part in the race, you can create your own ultrarunning experience using the extensive trails in the region.

40

SPAIN
MALLORCA
DRY STONE ROUTE

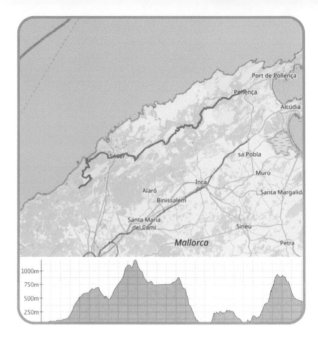

Start	Pollença, Spain
Overnight	Sóller, Spain
End	Valldemossa, Spain
Distance	43 miles / 69 kilometers
Elevation	+10,787 feet / +3 288 meters

Getting There

I took a direct flight to Mallorca, Spain from Berlin, Germany, and started the Dry Stone Route (GR-221) by taking a taxi to Pollença, where I could pick up the trail.

Liked Most

The Dry Stone Route is my favorite running destination because of its combination of mountain elevation, ocean views, friendly people, unique history, and quaint Spanish towns. The trail was well marked, well maintained, and runnable, with amazing variation in the terrain, especially the dry stone track that made its way up the mountain via switchbacks.

Unusual or Unique

What made this run amazing was the long dry stone pathway for the descent into Sóller. The trail was well maintained, but there were spots where the sides had crumbled away, leaving no barrier to several hundred-foot sheer drops. Also, the trail wound directly into town, transitioning from a mountain path to narrow village streets in a short distance.

Trail Description

The Dry Stone Route, also known as the GR-221, winds through the stunning landscapes of Mallorca, Spain. The trail takes you through diverse terrains, from flat country roads and trails following a stream to steep mountain inclines and switchbacks that showcase the area's unique dry stone tracks.

During the second day, you'll get to climb two mountains, the first offering expansive views of the ocean and steep cliffs, while the second showcases the impressive dry stone terraces. These terraces were built by generations of families between 900-1200 AD, offering a glimpse into the area's rich history and human drive. The trail meanders through these terraces via switchbacks, giving you the chance to appreciate the skill and effort that went into their construction.

While There

Stay at the Ecocrier hotel, where the owners are friendly and accommodating. Enjoy the sights and sounds of the ocean from the cliffs, and take time to appreciate the terraces and the amazing history they represent.

Unforgettable Experiences

While I won't forget any of these adventures, one experience that really stands out is this trip to Mallorca. In the past, when people have asked me what my favorite place to run is, I didn't have a good answer. However, now that I've run the Dry Stone Route in Mallorca, Spain, I have to say its combination of mountain elevation, ocean views, friendly people, unique history, and quaint Spanish towns have made it my favorite running destination so far. That being said, I'll never stop exploring and hope that each run challenges the Dry Stone Route as my favorite.

TRAIL END

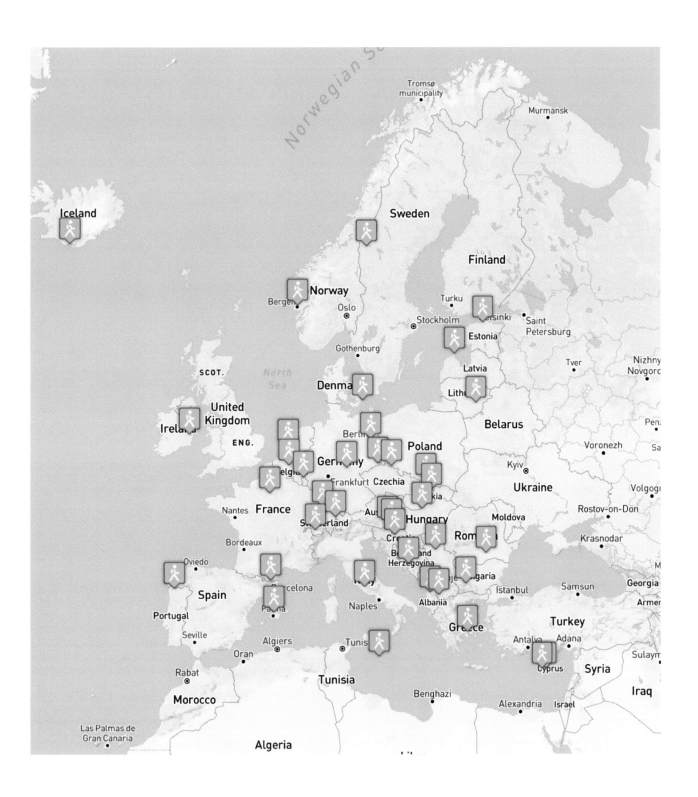

Printed in Great Britain
by Amazon

35115644R00094